YES U ARE!

The door bell rings, and there he is Mr. Postman bringing you a bunch of correspondence, yes, telephone bills, fast food propaganda, bank receipts, more bills, but suddenly between such desolation, something that brings a smile to your face: an invitation card!

Although we live in the digital age "par excellence" and the fact of receiving hundreds of emails is something really ordinary in our everyday lives, but we all really need the feel to touch something with our hands and smell the familiar scent of a letter paper. And there's nothing like the feeling of breaking an envelope!

We have showcased on this book a comprehensive selection of eye-catching invitations with infinite formats, original do-it-yourself concepts, detailed treatments, unconventional shapes, special finishing techniques, eco-friendly materials, cool hot stamping, unique materials, stickers, hot embossing, folded or inside non-conventional packages, amusing pop-up designs, cross-stitching, beautiful illustrated envelops, and great handmade fonts.

U R INVITED is an interesting inspiration source collection of memorable printed invitations by the hand of some of the most talented designers in the international design industry. A wedding? An upcoming car presentation? A private party? A fashion show? A museum exhibition? Yes, you are invited! There's no excuse, it's time to celebrate!

# AHOY

LET'S SET SAIL, SEPTEMBER TWENTY-SEVENTH FOR
AN EVENING OF COCKTAILS, CLAMS AND LOBSTER.
COCKTAILS BEGIN *at* FIVE. DINNER SERVED *at* SEVEN.

1760 ENTERPRISE PARKWAY ||| TWINSBURG OHIO 44087

SINCE 1924

SEA YOU SOON

OLIVER PRINTING COMPANY
1760 ENTERPRISE PARKWAY
TWINSBURG OHIO
44087

## AN EVENING OF CLAMBAKING
D: Christine Wisnieski
C: Oliver Printing Company

Taking inspiration from the age
when less was more, the Oliver
Printing Company identity was
founded on the concept of a single
letter form. For the company's
thirty-second annual clambake, a
crafted foiled stamped invitation
was designed, a gable style favor
box and a set of sea-inspired but-
tons to share with guests.

Invitation for Red Oak collection
show presentation. Hot stamping
over brown savanna paper and red
popset paper with special die cut.

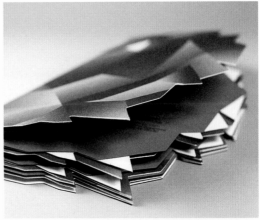

BOMBAY SAPPHIRE7CDC
D: Musa Work Lab
C: Moda Lisboa

7th Bombay Sapphire glass design
contest invitation. Offset printing
and hot stamping over curious
silver with special die cutter.

**UNDER THE OAK TREE**
D: Silent Partner
C: Suzy and Shane Tuxen

For these invitations, a bespoke
industrial typeface was crafted
based on a signage. Ryan Ward
of United Measures and friend of
Silent Partner was commissioned
to screen-print onto American Oak
tablets referencing their coming
together "under the oak tree."

THANK YOU

SUZY & SHANE

SUZY & SHANE

DETAILS

## THE SAILOR AND THE MERMAID
D: Until Sunday
C: Private client

Francesco and Ivana hired Until Sunday creative agency to design their wedding invitation. It was their wish to have as a main theme their passion for the sea. They produced an original invitation, ship-shaped, fully illustrated and printed in just one color. During the reception, 155 bottles of wine were given to the guests as a good omen for the young couple. Each bottle had been labelled and numbered individually by hand. On the neck of the bottle there was a small gold sticker telling how, in the past, wine was used to inaugurate the new boats instead of the most expensive champagne.

Francesco & Ivana
annunciano con gioia il loro matrimonio
Chiesa S. Agata al COLLEGIO
corso umberto 1, caltanissetta
3 settembre 2010, ore 16:00

La RICCHEZZA DEL MIO CUORE
è INFINITA COME IL MARE
COSÌ PROFONDO IL MIO AMORE:
PIÙ te ne do, PIÙ ne ho,
PERCHÉ entrambi SONO INFINITI.

William Shakespeare

Letterpress printed wedding invitations completed with a tide calendar of the couple, Jasen and Jackie, who love surf, dive, and spearfish.

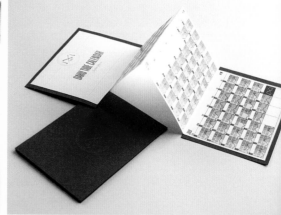

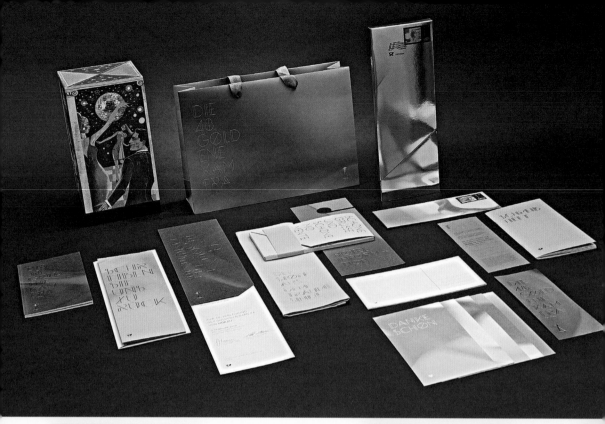

## HÖRZU'S 48TH GOLDEN CAMERA
D: PaperLux™
C: Axel Springer AG

For the 48th awards presentation of the Golden
Camera from HÖRZU, Paperlux decided to go for
gray and explore its sophisticated diversity, which
is often unfairly overshadowed in everyday life.
Furnished with a font made exclusively for the
event, their gala-gray appeared on various natural
paper varieties in countless shades of gray with
extreme horizontal formatting. Using macro
photography, the shadows of the Golden Camera
trophy continue into the background and are
refined with iriodin lacquer finishing. The stamp,
which has been exclusively designed for this
event, is black and also exhibits an iriodin finish.
They created a cloth napkin invitation for the es-
corts of the guests and the packaging delivered a
dazzling debut with its metal-coated material and
golden hot foil embossing. All images are from the
photographer Michael Pfeiffer.

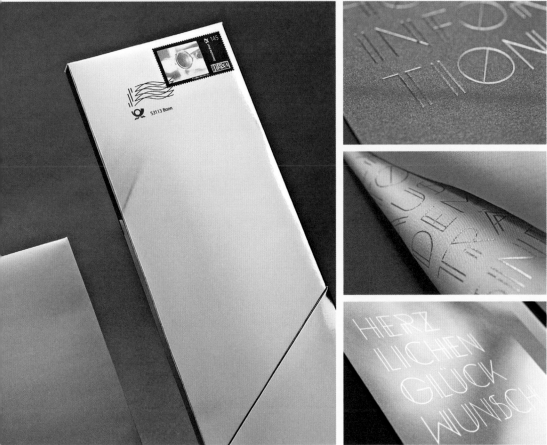

MOËT & CHANDON
TERÁ O PRAZER DA SUA COMPANHIA NA

# MOËT & CHANDON/
# FÊTE D'OR/ uma noite de esplendor.

/sexta-feira,
/13 de junho 2008
/22 horas

/Casa de Serralves
/Porto

Dress Code / Convite pessoal e intransmissível. / RSFF até 10 de junho
Toque de Ouro / Apresentação obrigatória. / T. 912 151 606
/ moet@moetportugal.com

« Entrada na Casa de Serralves através da Av. Marechal Gomes da Costa »

MOËT & CHANDON
CHAMPAGNE

MOËT & CHANDON FÊTE D'OR
D: Musa Work Lab
C: Moët & Chandon

Invitation for Moët & Chandon party. One
color offset printing over gold paper, folded
and closed with a strap.

NIKE HUMAN RACE
D: Popocorn Design
C: Nike

Nike approached to Popocorn Design creatives with a brief
to create a VIP package that they could mail to celebrities
encouraging them to take part in the UK leg of the Nike Human
Race. The VIP mailer consists of a uniquely number running vest,
Nike+SportBand, socks and an invitation. They scoured the land
and sourced the perfect box which mimicked the SportBand's
packaging design. To add that extra premium quality they hand
finished each item, applied a silver foil swoosh to the front of the
invitation and custom Nike stickers to seal the lid.

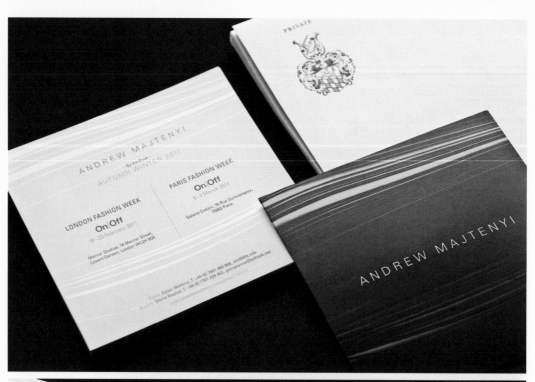

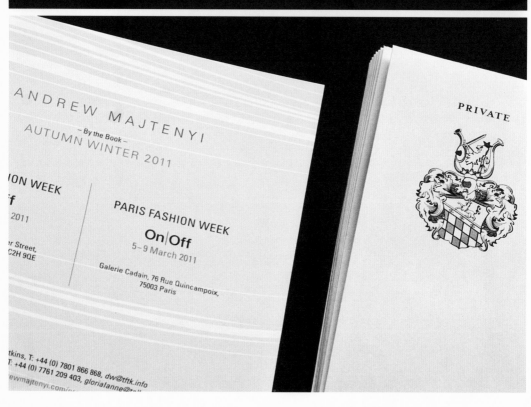

COURT ROAD, LONDON SW5 9FE UNITED KINGDOM

PRIVATE

LONDON & PARIS FASHION WEEK
D: Sascha Hass @Pylon Design
C: Andrew Majtenyi

Fashion Designer Andrew Majtenyi named his autumn/winter collection "By the books" and asked to Pylon Design to design marketing collaterals for the London and Paris Fashion week, such as private invitations for the runway shows. Based on his inspiration they took photographs of pages, flipping through a book and used these as graphic elements. The lines created the base of the invitation. Using varnish and matt as a finish the overall look is sophisticated, elegant and underlines the style of his collections.

Shinsaibashi Plaza bldg 1F  3-12-12 Minami Senba Chuo-ku, Osaka    www.louisvuitton.com

# LOUIS VUITTON

LOUIS VUITTON ORIGAMI
D: Happy Centro
C: Louis Vuitton

Happy Centro was asked to design and produce the
invitation card for a new Louis Vuitton' store opening
in Osaka, Japan. The starting idea was a paper object
inspired on the expression of perpetual precision
and pureness of the origami world, and mixed with
Happy Centro's intimate passion for special printing
techniques.

With a sincere appreciation of Marfa's culture and purpose, the Texas town was selected as the location for the first satellite extension of Oklahoma's City Arts Center. The new gallery plans were well underway when Ghost was approached to help create an identity for the venture; the type of project every designer dreams of. Client wanted a high-end invitation for their first exhibit. The result was a minimal approach that included a heavy card stock, debossing and clear foil.

# LIKE A VIRGIN

ELECTRONIC SUNDAYS
D: Serial Cut™
C: Goa Electronic Parties

For almost twenty years, Goa has been the best monthly Sunday party in Madrid. An outstanding selective international music program and excessive attention to every last detail has been the secret to becoming its being a classic and a reference point. The last rebranding and visual work defined the different themes of each party. All images are from artist and photographer Bartholot.

# THE SEPTEMBER ISSUE
## OPENING PARTY

## ROCKY HORROR SHOW
### HALLOWEEN

## NAKED
### XVII ANIVERSARIO

# MADRIZ ME PUEDE
## IX EDICIÓN

## SUPERGOA

## FIN DEL MUNDO
### AÑO NUEVO 2012

## CELEBRITIES
### CARNAVAL

# ROCKSTAR
## CLOSING PARTY

28

MY PLEASURE
18 ANIVERSARIO

MY PLEASURE ♦♦
AÑO NUEVO 2013

MY PLEASURE
18 ANIVERSARIO

The designer Alson Low designed this invitation for his 22nd birthday party. The theme for the party was: Cool Black. Low sent out the invitation together with the details to the party and a DIY spectacles attached inside. To hype up the event, he had windmills to decorate the place. Low also did a Polaroid cover and a "glad you came" sticker to thank his guests for attending to his party.

GREY GOOSE INVITES
D: Musa Work Lab
C: Grey Goose

Digital invitations designed for
Grey Goose vodka private parties.

Four
Thursday
Nights
Four
DJ's
Sets

DJ SET BY:
XANA
GUERRA

Serão apresentados no Bed Room
os cocktails **Grey Goose Spicy**
e **Grey Goose Dragon.**

QUINTA-FEIRA
**5 MARÇO 23H**

**GREY GOOSE**
World's Best Tasting Vodka

Bed ROOM

SEJA RESPONSÁVEL. BEBA COM MODERAÇÃO.

DJ SET BY:
NINFETA CATITA
E EL PINTON

Serão apresentados no Bed Room
os cocktails **Grey Goose White**
e **Twilight Chocolat.**

QUINTA-FEIRA
**12 MARÇO 23H**

**GREY GOOSE**
World's Best Tasting Vodka

Bed ROOM

SEJA RESPONSÁVEL. BEBA COM MODERAÇÃO.

Four
Thursday
Nights
Four
DJ's
Sets

DJ SET BY:
CÁTIA
CASTEL-BRANCO
& CONVIDADOS

Serão apresentados no Bed Room
os cocktails **Grey Goose Cosmopolitan**
e **Grey Goose French Caribbean.**

QUINTA-FEIRA
**2 ABRIL 23H**

**GREY GOOSE**
World's Best Tasting Vodka

Bed ROOM

SEJA RESPONSÁVEL. BEBA COM MODERAÇÃO.

Four
Thursday
Nights
Four
DJ's
Sets

DJ SET BY:
SARA
AVELINO

Serão apresentados no Bed Room
os cocktails **Grey Goose Platine**
e **Grey Goose Indian Sunset.**

QUINTA-FEIRA
**19 MARÇO 23H**

Bed ROOM

SEJA RESPONSÁVEL. BEBA COM MODERAÇÃO.

LOVE SWEET LOVE
D: Binocular Studio
C: Alba + Jordi

For Alba and Jordi's wedding, the designers from Binocular Studio were able to create an identity for a one-day-event. The aim was to create a fresh and romantic style, mixing the vintage style with the modern and that was present on each detail and on every corner, from the "save the date" expression to the invitations design, the menu, the fans, the signage, petals, note papers and also in the photobooth poster.

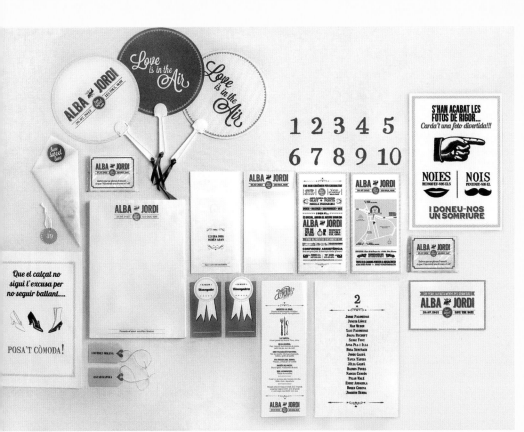

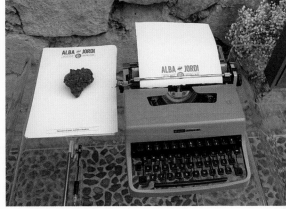

ALESSANDRA & DAVID CHOCOLATE
D: Gummy Industries
C: David Saitta

This cute packaging, handfolded on about
two hundred Novi's chocolate bars, was
designed for Alessandra & David's wedding.
Every invitation contains a map to reach the
church and a funny rhyme about the special
occasion.

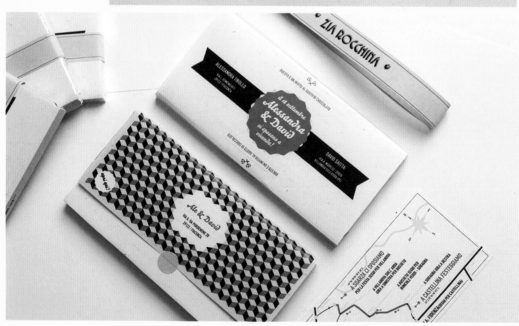

2<sup>ND</sup> BIRTH-D SAVE THE DATE
D: D-Studio
C: D-Studio

At D-Studio they like a good party and they don't often
need an excuse to celebrate one. To celebrate that the
design agency was turning into two, they threw a party of
2-D proportions. Having already sent out an eye test style
save the date, they referenced the classic 3-D glasses from
yesteryear for the main invite by sending a variety of cut-
out-and-make glasses, inviting their guests to come and see
their 2-D spectacular, comprising a world of two-dimensional
items, which included a bear rug, a chandelier, a deer head,
floor lamps, picture frames and even a 2-D butler to welcome
their esteemed guests.

# 25
# OCT
# 2012
# HOPE
## TO SEE YOU
## AT OUR 2ND
### BIRTHDAY PARTY
#### INVITE TO FOLLOW SOON

20 / 200

20 / 100

20 / 70

20 / 50

20 / 40

20 / 20

20 / 15

20 / 12

d.

ES CAU
D: Lluís Serra
C: Es Cau Restaurant

This plate-postcard is part of a "tapa tasting" promotion whereby tapas
were offered to passers-by in the street to promote Es Cau, an small restaurant in Cadaqués, a beautiful town in the province of Girona, Catalonia,
Spain. Specialising in natural, home grown products, the restaurant offers
a wide choice of natural dishes, suitable for both vegetarians and vegans.
Once the tapa has been eaten, the passer-by is left with a postcard an-
nouncing the opening of the restaurant.

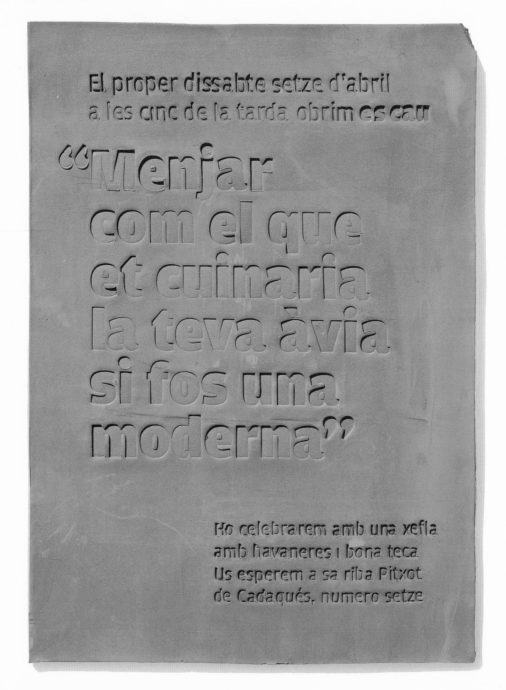

El proper dissabte setze d'abril
a les cinc de la tarda obrim es cau

"Menjar
com el que
et cuinaria
la teva àvia
si fos una
moderna"

Ho celebrarem amb una xefla
amb havaneres i bona teca.
Us esperem a sa riba Pitxot
de Cadaqués, numero setze

El proper dissabte setze d'abril
a les cinc de la tarda obrim es cau

"Menjar ràpid sense presses"

Aperitius i tapes de la terra, hamburgueses de la casa, bio i vegan; frankfurts i embotits alemanys i productes frescos i de temporada
Ho celebrarem amb una xefla amb havaneres i bona teca
Us esperem a sa riba Pitxot de Cadaqués, número setze

El proper dissabte setze d'abril
a les cinc de la tarda obrim es cau

"un fast fut a la nostra manera"

Aperitius i tapes de la terra, hamburgueses de la casa, bio i vegan; frankfurts i embotits alemanys i productes frescos i de temporada
Ho celebrarem amb una xefla amb havaneres i bona teca
Us esperem a sa riba Pitxot de Cadaqués, número setze

El proper dissabte setze d'abril
a les cinc de la tarda obrim es cau

"Menjar ràpid sense presses"

Aperitius i tapes de la terra, hamburgueses de la casa, bio i vegan; frankfurts i embotits alemanys i productes frescos i de temporada
Ho celebrarem amb una xefla amb havaneres i bona teca
Us esperem a sa riba Pitxot de Cadaqués, número setze

El proper dissabte setze d'abril
a les cinc de la tarda obrim es cau

"un fast fut a la nostra manera"

Aperitius i tapes de la terra, hamburgueses de la casa, bio i vegan; frankfurts i embotits alemanys i productes frescos i de temporada
Ho celebrarem amb una xefla amb havaneres i bona teca
Us esperem a sa riba Pitxot de Cadaqués, número setze

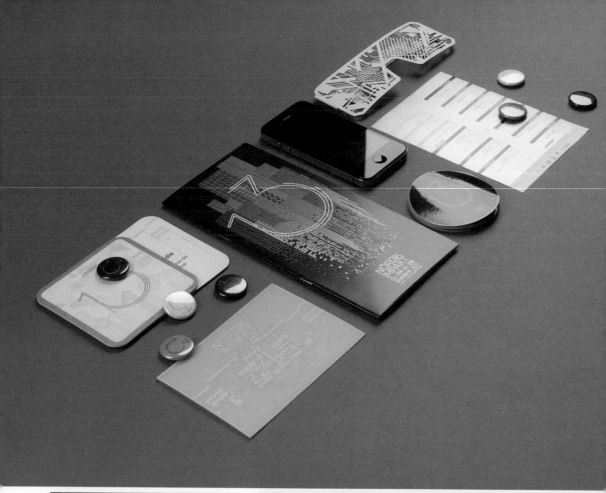

## NÖRDIK IMPAKT 13 COLLECTOR EDITION
### D: Murmure
### C: The Nördik Impakt Festival

The Nordik Impakt festival, nocturnal electronic music event, communicates around
limited and collector goodies. Murmure
agency, for this event, developed conceptual
products around electronic music and phos-
phorescence. They came up with supports
with two reading levels. The agency made
posters and invitation cards which extend
the graphic design, and reveals its electronic
spirit when the light goes out. The agency
unveils a concept with a totally innovative
design by creating electro-phosphorescent
glasses made out of paper.

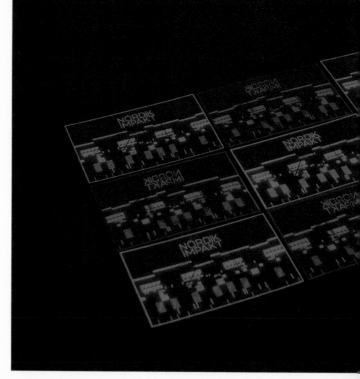

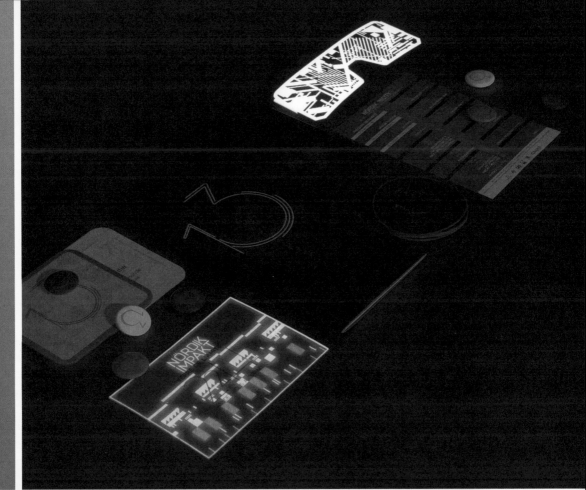

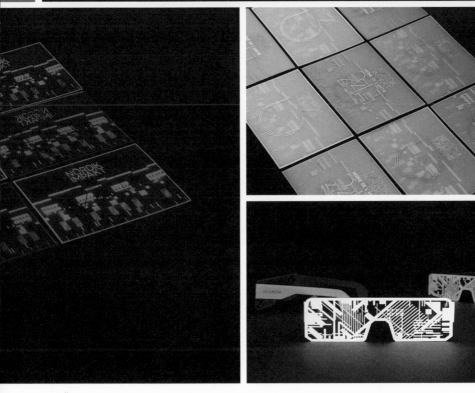

Many couples have a song that links them. In the case of Patricia and Gian this link is Jack Jonshon`s song "Better togheter." The idea behind the invitation is to communicate the wedding details playing with the chorus of this song. A funny and unusual method was thought for discovering the details of the wedding. The guests themselves reveal the nal message via scratching-o the golden ink. The wedding details this appear interspersed in the chorus of the Jack Johnson's song.

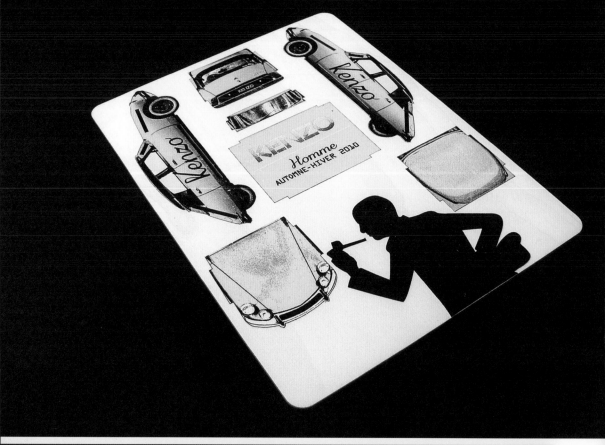

The Kenzo fall/winter 2010 show was inspired by "Traffic"
movie by french director Jacques Tati, the invitation was a
Citroen DS miniature made as a constructible wooden toy.
During the runway show finale, Kenzo models parade around
the "Place des Victoires" in Paris, surrounded by 30 vintage
Citroen DS in different colors.

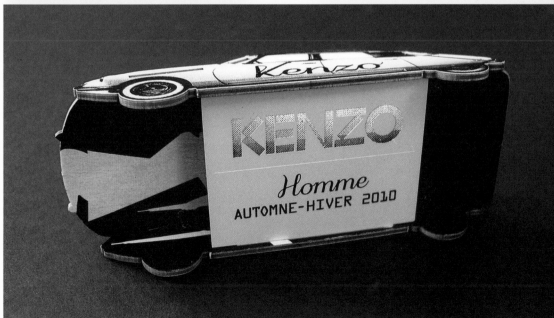

EUROPEAN MUSEUM NIGHT
D: Murmure
C: Caen's Museum of Fine Arts

For the European Night of Museums of
2011, the museum of Fine Arts of Caen
entrusted Murmure with the task of
developing the conceptual planning
of the event celebrated in the castle
gardens. Light, transparency and poetry
are the themes which inspired Murmure.
They designers suggested an street-mar-
keting concept: luminous balloons
transporting the invitation cards floated
across the streets of the town. A black
envelope revealed its content using
transparence and attracting the visitor
to the gardens to discover a luminous
and ethereal installation.

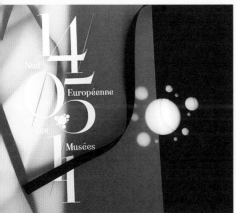

/ Musée des Beaux-Arts de Caen

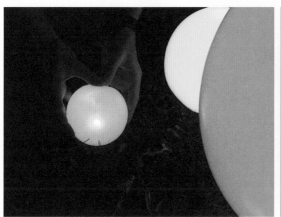

Invitation set inspired by the couple's love for all Britain thing and vintage typography. The invitation folder contained a collection of cards with all the information that guests needed for their wedding-tea-party. The cards, in different formats informed people of the where, the what, and the what to wear. The folder also contained a tea-bag sewn into the paper. At the party all items were also design to accompany the look and feel of the invitation.

KENZO BUTTERFLY INVITE
D: Paolo Bazzni
C: Kenzo

Inspired by *Alice in wonderland* the invite was a botanic journal book, with a surprising flower pop-up. The runway show also was made of oversized pop-up books that opened up during the fashion show finale.

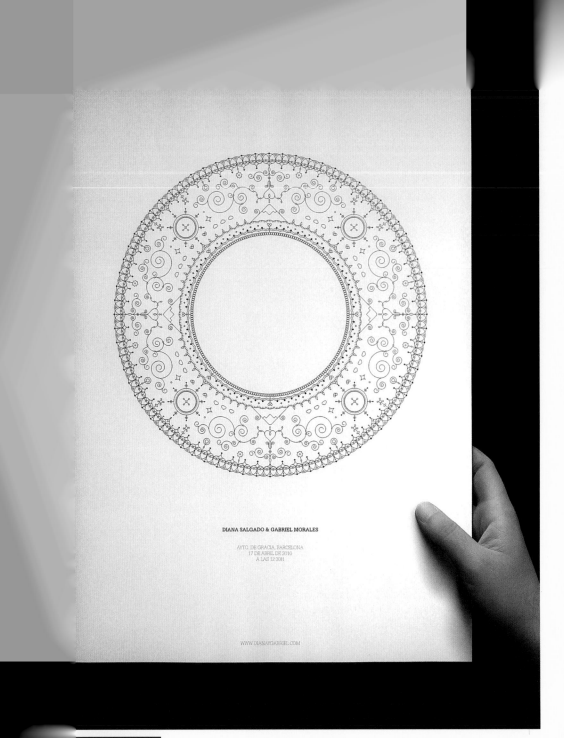

DIANA SALGADO & GABRIEL MORALES

AYTO. DE GRACIA, BARCELONA
17 DE ABRIL DE 2010
A LAS 12:30H.

WWW.DIANAYGABRIEL.COM

DIANA & GABRIEL
D: Dorian
C: Private Client

Wedding invitation focussed on the most
significant element of the union: the
alliance. Built through a universe inspired
by the ornamental iconography of the 19th
century, the illustrations of this alliance
represent the most characteristic aspects of
the couple.

Direct mailer for Popcorn Design inviting their clients to experience beautiful print process which they don't often see. They chose letterpress as the process for the typographic designs, printed colour printed on 600gsm Saunders 100% cotton stock paper.

53

Getxophoto is a photography festival in Getxo, Basque Country, Spain. The 2011 theme for this event was "In Praise of Elderly," and the brief was to create a graphic image for the exhibition representing the elderly on a simple but not very serious way. For the design of the invitations the studio thought that the cross-stitching was a great idea to represent it. The invitation came with a needle and a thread to connect the dots with the thread to understand the message. The lines were shaping the number 5 because of the fifth edition of this festival.

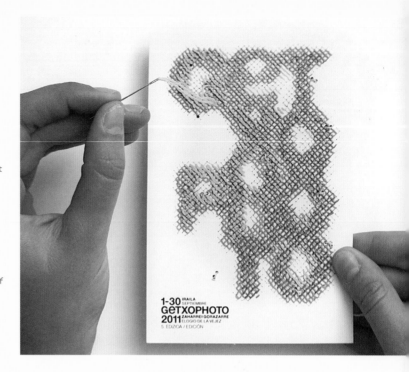

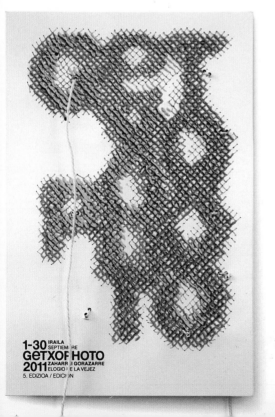

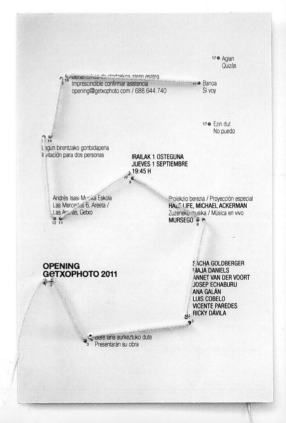

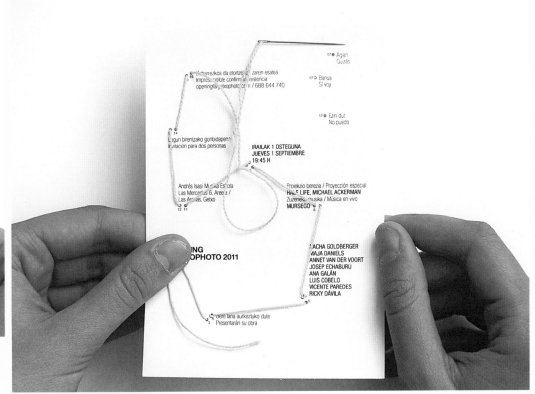

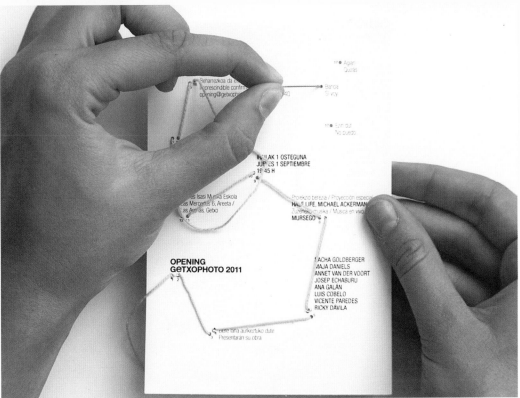

This design and illustration printing for
a wedding invitation was made using an
offset ledger paper. The poster was folded
and inserted on a Manila paper envelope, tied
with a red waxed thread.

NME AWARDS VIP INVITATION
D: Popcorn Design
C: New Musical Express

VIP invitation design for the 2011 NME
(New Musical Express) Awards. This invite
involved the designers to source original 7"
indie vinyls and overprinting the labels with
bespoke stickers which detailed the events
information.

A ERIC KAYSER
TÊM O PRAZER
DE CONVIDAR

PARA O COCKTAIL
DE INAUGURAÇÃO
NO DIA 20 SETEMBRO
ENTRE AS 19:30H
E AS 22:00H.

DJ SET BY MARY B

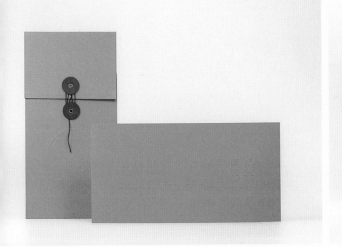

ERIC KAYSER
ARTISAN BOULANGER
—— PARIS ——

Amoreiras Plaza
R. Prof. Carlos Alberto da Mota Pinto
Lisboa

ERIC KAYSER AMOREIRAS
D: Musa Work Lab
C: Eric Kayser

Invitation for the opening party of the first
French Eric Kayser boulangerie in Lisboa,
Portugal. Following the brand color code,
invitations were printed in a curious orange
skin paper with detailed finishings such as
black hot stamped text, foil embossed logo
and fastened with a string.

THE CORDIAL INVITATIONS
D: K D Dixon
C: Self Authored

These invites were originated as a set of notes called "Personal Reminders When Making", a sort of the designer's personal check list to keep him in line during the creative process. After receiving a generous amount of help from his creative community, he wanted to send out a thank you gift which could be passed on by the recipient, continuing the communal spirit. He transformed his list of "Personal Reminders" into type studies and packaged them as a postcard set, the Cordial Invitations–to makers.

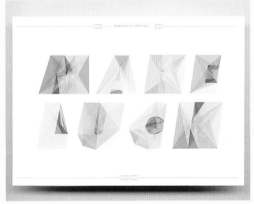

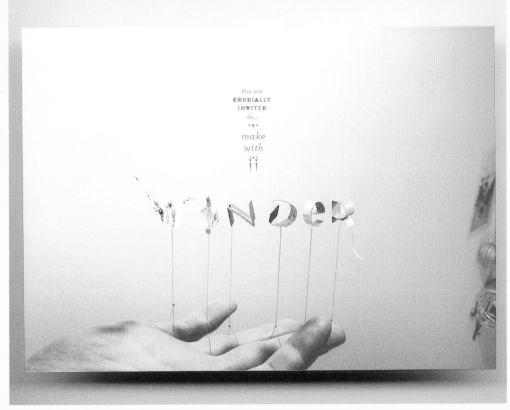

RICARD & MARTA'S WEDDING
D: Bildi Grafiks
C: Ricard + Marta

The studio designed this special chocolate
box as an original wedding invitation.
A letter was concealed beneath each
chocolate, and when all the chocolates
were eaten, the complete message was
revealed. The invitation thus became a
gift for the invited guests as well as a
very sweet way of inviting them to be
part of the special day.

## CAMP'S INVITATION
**D: Paprika**
**C: Domison**

Invitation for Camp's bar and restaurant opening. During that period of time, many restaurants were opening their doors. Journalist, cook critics and many other personalities were receiving invitations to go taste the new menus freshly arrived in town. To distinguish themselves, Paprika studio created a very large format of invitation: a very big poster that when unfolded gives a certain impact on customer's curiosity.

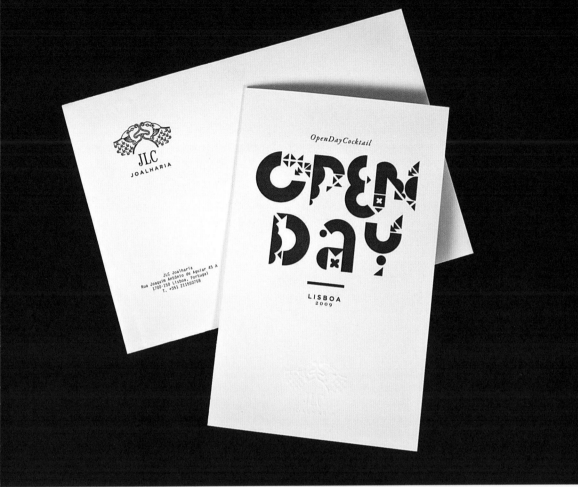

JLC
D: Musa Work Lab
C: JLC Joalhoaria

Invitation for jewelry collection presentation opening day. Printed on saville row plain paper with blind emboss.

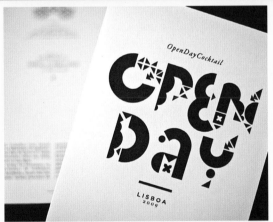

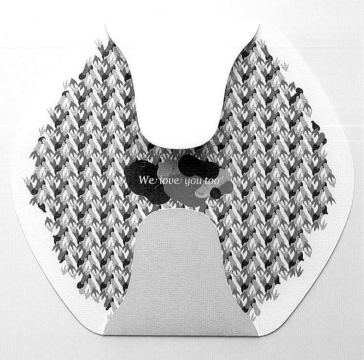

## WEDDING INVITATION
D: José Mendes @Maga
C: Private client

José Mendes at Maga Studio, designed
this cute invitation for Inês and Hugo's
wedding. The names of the couple have
been mixed to perfection on a lovely
typographic illustration. The envelope is
closed with a purple wax seal stamp.

Robert Geller is an award-winning menswear fashion brand based in New York. Photographer Sarah Moon's moody, painterly images of beaches were a touchstone for the spring/summer 2013 collection. Studio NewWork were assigned to design this show invitation and their graphic solution was to use a foggy and blurry image to represent the theme with a playful placement of the typography.

LYDIA DELGADO LA FÊTE
D: Sonsoles Llorens
C: Lydia Delgado

Invitation for Lydia Delgado's fashion show.
The extra thick material and the die brings
to this piece the quality and audacity of this
Spanish fashion designer.

Invitation for an exhibition at the
Montreal Museum of Fine Arts–MBAM
(Musée des Beaux Arts de Montréal).
The idea was to take over the concept
of supermarket receipts. The receipt
was stapled to the invitation a pass
to visit the event. The final design was
linked to the exhibition completely.

BIG APPLE
D: Sasha Prood
C: Madewell

This multi-piece apple invitation was a playful way to bring editors to Madewell's spring 2011 collection preview, which was themed after the "Big Apple."

YOU'RE INVITED

Be the first to see Madewell's
SPRING '11 COLLECTION
(inspired by the amazing style seen on the
streets of our hometown, the Big Apple).

NOVEMBER 11TH, 9–11AM
770 BROADWAY, NEW YORK CITY

RSVP: meaghan.curcio@madewell.com

THERE'S A TREAT
FOR YOU INSIDE.
Open soon, it's fresh!

This apple was
handpicked for you
at New York's
Red Jacket Orchards.

EARLY BIRDS GET THE WORM. We'll be serving NYC-inspired breakfast bites starting at 9am.

YOU'RE INVITED

Be the first to see Madewell's
SPRING '11 COLLECTION
(inspired by the amazing style seen on the
streets of our hometown, the Big Apple).

NOVEMBER 11TH, 9–11AM
770 BROADWAY, NEW YORK CITY

RSVP: meaghan.curcio@madewell.com

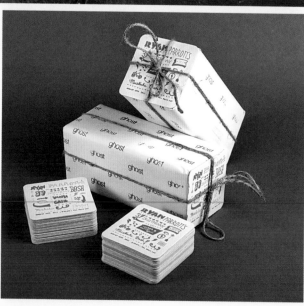

## IGUANA MEXICAN GRILL
### D: Ghost
### C: Iguana Mexican Grill

The request for this project was to create 100 unique invitations for the head chef of the popular Iguana Mexican Grill. It was his 37th birthday and the restaurant was throwing a party together with Automobile Alley's Mustache Bash. The solution proposed were individually silk-screened coasters that could be given out and be used. They liked the idea so much that they upped the quantity to 2,500. A couple of cases of Stella and several late nights later, Ghost delivered the finished coasters that thrilled the chef and helped pack out the party.

D: Alvaro Villarrubia & Fernando Vicente
C: Pacha Ibiza

The renowned photographer Álvaro Villarrubia
and the Illustrator Fernando Vicente worked
together on the artwork for these invitations for
the 40th anniversary for legendary's Pacha Ibiza
club. The inspiration was based on the art of
René Grau, specially on the artwork poster he did
for The Lido and The Moulin Rouge, both in Paris,
in the late 50s and 60s.

Invitation and identity materials for
Mamastudio's 10th birthday celebration.
The slogan for this special year's event was
DayNight and for the website they chose
a playground, perfect for both the picnic
and the night attractions. The bat was
chosen as this edition's mascot and symbol,
appearing in the advertising media in two
versions, valid both for day and night. The
bat was awake or asleep depending which
way you turned the invitation or poster.

79

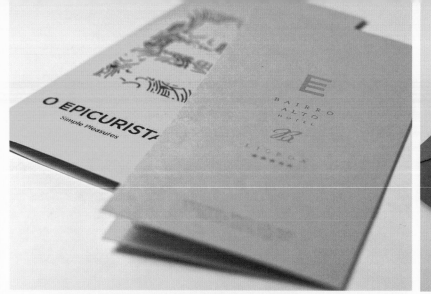

EPICURISTA OPENING DAY
D: Musa Work Lab
C: Epicurista

Invitation series for the opening party of two Epicurista stores in Lisboa, Portugal. The invitations were offset and silk-screened printed over fine papers. Detailed hot stamping texts and custom-die cuts gave this exclusive final finishing touch.

COUNTING DOWN THE DAYS

MARK & DANIELA

DAYS TO GO

11·07
2012

SICILY ♥ ITALY

TO CELEBRATE

www.markanddany...

M ♥
D ♥
HOME
SWEET
HOME
♠ a
♠ M

NG DOWN THE DAYS

ULY

DAYS TO GO

MARK & DANIELA

MARCH

In 2012, a happy couple, a Sicilian bride and a Dutch groom, hired Until Sunday studio to design an invitation to announce their wedding. They were looking forward for that day for so long that the first thing that came out of the designer's mind was to create a sort of calendar. The invitation has on its front a wheel that counts down the days for the wedding. The "countdown" idea became very funny when a few weeks before the wedding, all the guests began to post the number of days left until the wedding on the bride and the groom's Facebook pages. The invitation is printed in two colors–red, symbolizing Sicily and orange, Dutch's national color–and printed over a Vintage paper by Arjo Wiggins. They also redesigned Sicily's flag symbol, the Medusa, by adding some tulips, The Netherland's symbolic flower.

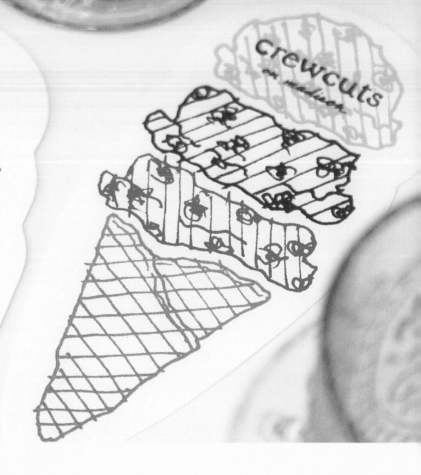

# HERE'S THE SCOOP...

ntroducing our new crewcuts
store on Madison Avenue.
one of the first to shop and
an exclusive gift* with any
chase of $100 or more.

## crewcuts
*on madison*

0 Madison Avenue
een 87th and 88th)
New York City

hile supplies last

This playful ice cream cone card and Yo-Yo
gift were designed to attract customers
to Crewcuts' Madison Avenue new store
opening. These items were handed out along
with a cup of delicious ice cream, dispensed
from a similarly styled cart, also designed by
Sasha Prood.

**GET TO THE TOP**
D: Musa WorkLab
C: Elite Model Look Portugal

Musa WorkLab were chosen to design this invitation for Elite Model Look in Portugal. The purple and black colors and the mixed fonts gives a clean and modern touch for this competition in search of new fashion model talents.

KENZO RUSSIA
D: Paolo Bazzni
C: Kenzo

The main inspiration for this Kenzo
fashion show invitation was Russian's
constructivism period. The invite was
made by five wooden cubes with
iconic symbols, people, and letters
from Russia.

THE COLLECTION RESTAURANT
D: Mind Design
C: The Collection Restaurant

The Collection is a restaurant, a cultural event, and a retail space. Mind Design designed the identity, signage system and all printed material. The idea for the identity relates to multiple prints, limited editions and artist signatures. The execution is relatively simple: Everything is based on an A5 format with punched holes. They used screen printing which allowed them to change colours on the printing bed and makes each print unique. Larger signs are made up by several A5 boards and the thickness is achieved by hanging several signs in front of each other. For the logo they asked the client to write the name in their own handwriting connecting two dots equivalent to the punched holes.

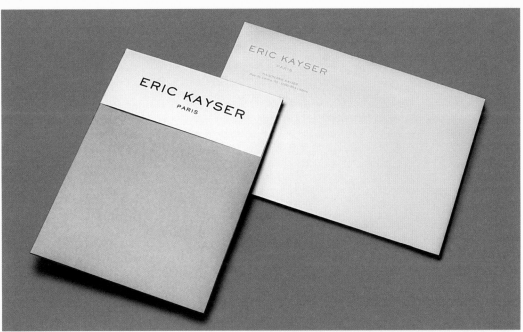

ERIC KAYSER PARIS
D: Musa Work Lab
C: Eric Kayser

Opening invitation for Eric Kayser's
second French boulangerie in Lisboa,
Portugal. Two color printed Munken paper,
folded to keep the main invitation inside.

## ORANGE BOAT
D: Despina Aeraki
C: Giota Gavogianni

The main idea for this project was an invitation-booklet offered to the guests inside a gift box. The client wrote and illustrated a fairytale and the designer painted it. In the fairytale, starring little Peter, he sails away into an orange boat; this gave the inspiration for the favor, which was shaped as a 3-D paper boat.

This invitation was sent out inviting guests to the Bone Growth Foundation fundraising dinner with themed around magic. A fun, interactive invitation made from brightly coloured silk scarves pulled from the tube it was delivered in—made from recycled material roll ends. The details magically appear at the end.

D: John Shepherd
C: MetroMedia

Owner and founder of MetroMedia, Paul Manning had set a precedence with big christmas parties, but this one was going to be massive. His brief was "Do what ever you want." A simple little christmas invite folds out into a large poster. The theme was "Christ-massive." And it was!

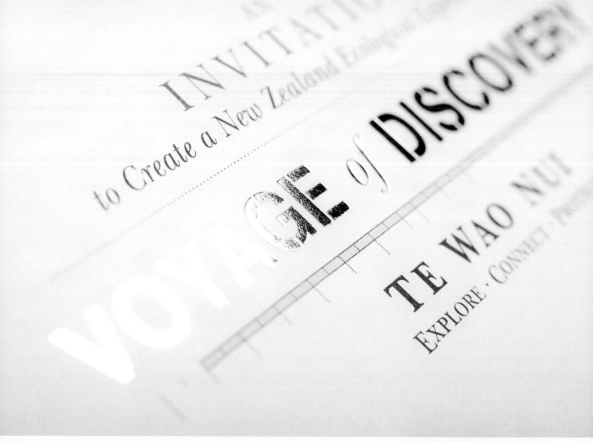

TE WAO NUI SPONSORSHIP
D: John Shepherd
C: Auckland Zoo

Inspired by the work of the ships artist onboard HMS Endeavour, Sydney Parkinson, whose work recorded Aotearoa -New Zealand's flora and fauna for the very first time. This document invited New Zealand trusts and corporations to be part of preserving, protecting and showcasing the nations natural treasures for generations to come by making a donation to the development.

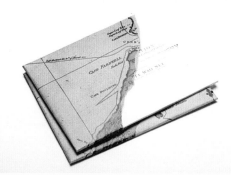

## 5

"I AM ABOUT TO SET OUT
## ON A LONG AND HAZARDOUS VOYAGE,
*from which God alone knows whether I shall ever return."*

In 1768, Scottish-born Sydney Parkinson boarded Captain James Cook's barque Endeavour as they set out for what became their initial maiden voyage to the Pacific.

Cook's role was that of captain and expedition leader. In contrast, Parkinson, with his skills as a botanical illustrator and natural history artist, was entrusted to record what he saw with his very own eyes.

During voyages, conditions were cramped and, being the perfectionists they were, ship's artists' work demands were intense.

Ship's artists produced thousands of drawings of flora and fauna. Sadly, some never returned home. However, their talents and efforts enabled a small, privileged audience outside of Aotearoa to marvel at our natural treasures for the very first time.

## 6

IT'S TIME TO
## SHOW OURSELVES TO THE WORLD
*Our creatures, plants, culture and history*

QUE VIVA KENZO
D: Paolo Bazzani
C: Kenzo

Inspired by Mexican pop culture, the invitation for this Kenzo fashion show was a
typical floral skull mask as the one made
for the iconic Day of the Dead.

WEDDING INVITATION
D: Popcorn Design
C: Tomoko & Kennzo

Design of a typographic contemporary wedding
invitation, appealing to both the young couple
and guests alike. Using the typeface Neo Deco,
this invitation was printed in gold on a 350gsm
Fedrigoni Arcoprint cardboard.

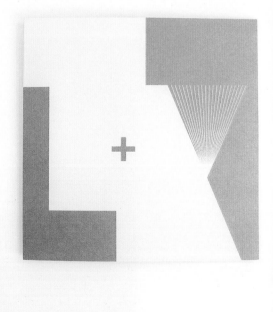

Tomoko Kawauchi
& Kennzo Southwell
are tying the knot

Please come join us
10.30am Saturday
24ª September 2011

Park Plaza Sherlock Holmes
108 Baker Street London
W1U 6LJ

**RSVP**
tomokogardens@gmail.com
E: 07702342574
T: 07945757072

Followed by an afternoon
tapas party
at the Oak from 12pm – 5pm

137 Westbourne Park Road,
London, W2 5QL

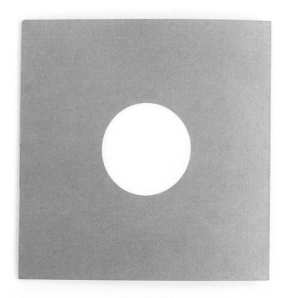

Leonor
e José Luis Barbosa
convidam para
a inauguração do
espaço b

14.10.2010 —
19h/23h —
DJ: Orson & Welles

Rua D. Pedro V, 120
Príncipe Real, Lisboa

RSFF: Armando Ribeiro
armandoribeiro@nbranddynamics.com

Nixon
Fred Perry
Converse
Timex 80
Nike

APC
Surface to Air
Histoires de Parfums
Thames&Hudson
VicMatié

Neil Barrett
Comme des Garçons
Maison Martin Margiela
KrisVanAssche
Marc Jacobs

espaço b

MODA · DESIGN · LIFESTYLE

ESPACIO B
D: Musa Work Lab
C: Espacio B

Invitation for Espacio B fashion store opening.
It was designed with a black acrylic silkscreen
with text on white color. The invitation goes
inside an engraved white PVC envelope.

BDD ANNUAL EVENT INVITE
D: Bunch Design
C: Brompton Design District

Invitation for Brompton Design District, an
annual event taking place in South Kensington,
London. Die-cut holes mark showroom activity.
Designed together with Schober Design.

PEARLS & PERFUMES EVENT INVITE
D: Bunch Design
C: Sylvia Gottwald & Institut Parfumeur Flores

PEARLS & PERFUMES EVENT INVITE
D: Bunch Design
C: Sylvia Gottwald & Institut Parfumeur Flores

Pearls & Perfumes was an collaboration event between
Sylvia Gottwald and Institut Parfumeur Flores. The
invitation uses holographic foil on a thick black card
in order to represent nacre in the closest possible way.
Sylvia's designs with pearls and nacre are unique pieces
in limited editions, created from seven species of pearl
producing shells, and various fresh water pearls.

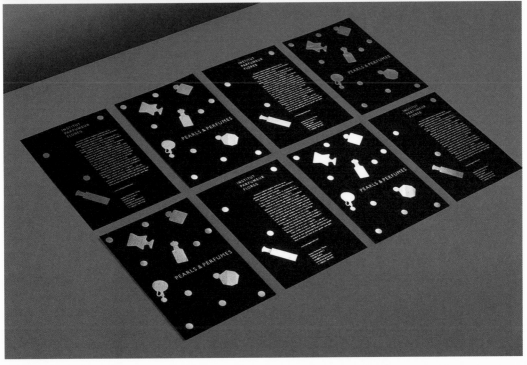

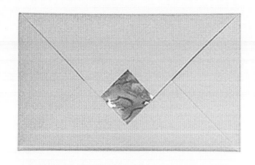

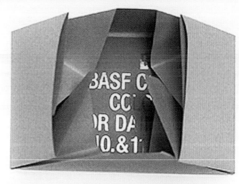

BESPOKE
D: Are We Designer
C: BASF Coatings GmbH

For this event a special theme has to be conceived that always accords to the annual Global Trend Book Theme, which in 2012 was "Wide Awake." For the annual workshop and Color Show 2012 all clients were invited to the Bespoke-Studio, where tailor-made color coatings were discussed and presented in a very special and classy atmosphere. Based on this concept invitations and additional event accessories such as name badges were handmade and customized on high class paper, refined with copper colored film plots and accurately fitting envelopes.

SCHRAUBEN SIE IHRE
ANSPRÜCHE HOCH!
BEI DER **BESPOKE**-
COLLECTION SOLL JEDES
DETAIL STIMMEN.

"Plant your Dreams and let them Grow" is the title of Sophia's self initiative project. The actual tulip flowers and their "unique" names–Pink Diamond or Sweetheart–inspired the designer to create a series of ecological packages containing tulip bulbs. The packages were sent as a gift to friends and clients offering a unique experience by telling them to "Plant their Dreams," take care of them and see if they will grow the next year. The illustrations on the packaging were inspired by the name of each "unique" tulip and were drawn by hand. All images are from the photographer Michalis Kloukinas.

78: THE CANNIEST DEGREE SHOW ON EARTH
D: Sean Ford
C: Northumbria Univeristy

Invitation for the Northumbria University 2012
Graphic Design Degree Show. The world of
circus was the theme chosen to convey the
family nature as well as the wide variety of
individual talents and characters that this large
year's group had. Titled "78" to represent each
exhibiting student from the course, the show
was centred around showing off all this talent
in a very informal and friendly way.

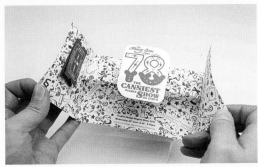

Hapag-Lloyd Cruises entrusted PaperLux™ to design a multi-stage invitation for the christening of the new MS EUROPA 2 luxury liner. For the "Save the Date" announcement, they chose a poster format with classic vaudeville motifs. Typography and color selections followed the corporate design, a classy finish in lustrous Iriodin emphasized the festive character of the event. For the reminder, they designed a card with satin ribbon, a small metal crank, and an overlying porthole in cardboard. The heart of the invitation that followed was a linen-covered box, which provided a view to a maritime landscape fashioned from paper. The attached crank sets waves, figurines and vaudeville performances in motion. The mechanism was developed in collaboration with set designer Tim John. The press invitation, with the figure of a photographer, was also designed as a visual box. For the packaging they used fine ropes and bowline knots—an additional homage to the MS EUROPA 2, which now travels the seas. All images are from the photographer Michael Pfeiffer.

## MAMMA FASHION SHOW
**D:** Paolo Bazzni
**C:** Antonio Marras

The whole collection was dedicated to Antonio
Marras' mother, so the invite was made with her
printed portrait with some flowers embroidered
with a red thread over her face.

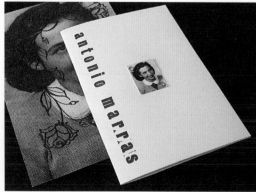

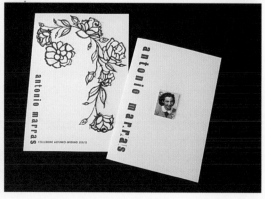

antonio marras

COLLEZIONE AUTUNNO INVERNO 2001/2

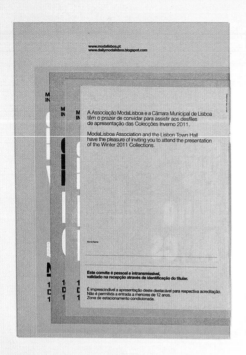

MODA LISBOA 34 CHECK POINT
D: Musa Work Lab
C: Moda Lisboa

Designers show, dinner and closing party invitations
for ModaLisboa 34th edition titled "Check Point".

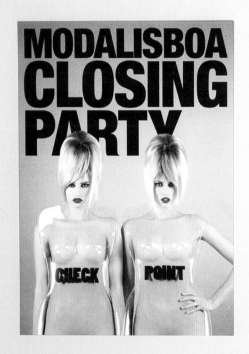

Invitation designed for Miss Sixty's collection show presentation. Full color printed and holographic hot stamping over curious metalics with special die cut and embossed. The invitation also included a badge for the after party admission.

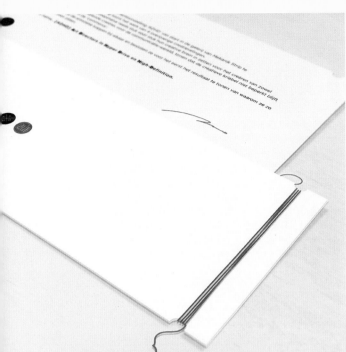

For the ADHD-Group exhibition in Antwerp a personal invitation was created in line with the work of one of its participants: Bruno Vergauwen. Like the limited portfolio's available at the opening night, the invitation used the red string as its key element. The design was minimalistic typo-wise and the guests could only discover the information by untangling the red string, holding the invite closed.

The Montreal Museum of Fine Arts is a major art museum in Montreal. After 150 years the Museum is growing with the addition of a new pavilion and the reinstallation of all of its collections. Paprika studio created the invitation for this event. Unfolded, the invitation let appear in paper and 3-D, the whole building which is a former church converted as a museum room and hall concert.

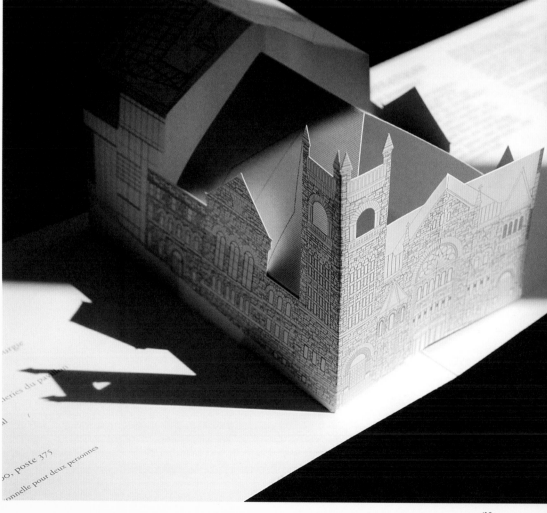

INVITATION XL
D: Paprika
C: Ballet Jazz de Montréal

Paprika Studio reviews the Les Ballets
Jazz de Montréal identity program
and also designed this invitation for
the company's 40th anniversary.

40ᵉ SOIRÉE BÉNÉFICE
SAMEDI LE 5 MAI 2012, 18H30
GALERIE L'ARSENAL
2020, RUE WILLIAM
GRIFFINTOWN, MONTRÉAL
SOUS LA PRÉSIDENCE
D'HONNEUR DE MONSIEUR
ANDREW T. MOLSON
RÉSERVEZ CETTE DATE
À VOTRE AGENDA
TENUE DE SOIRÉE

40
ans
bjm

ANNUAL GALA
DAY MAY 5TH 2012
ENAL GALLERY
20, WILLIAM
RIFFINTOWN, MONTR
UNDER THE HONOR
CHAIRMANSHIP
OF MR. ANDREW
RESERVE THIS
IN YOUR AGE
BLACK TIE

XL

MISSION DESIGN TAIPEI
D: Paprika
C: Mission Design

For the 2017 Montreal World Summit and Congress invitation, Paprika Studio took their inspiration from one of the host city's well-known icons. No surprise in an urban environment where the road less travelled is the one always under construction. The orange of the traffic cones and the Interstate font used for road signs simply imposed themselves. They also made an origami nod for their Asia friends since the folded invitation were distributed during the 2011 Taipei World Design Expo.

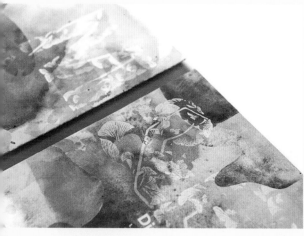

Invitation and CD sleeve designed for the Australian bush wedding of Meg and Ben. The couple, a horticulturist and a naturopath, have a shared history with the ancient ginkgo tree, choosing to give them as a bomboniere, this inspired a bespoke lettering treatment and watercolour artwork. The invites were printed with a raised thermographic ink to create a textural finish. The envelopes, CD's and belly bands were individually hand-stamped by the couple themselves to add a warm and more personal touch.

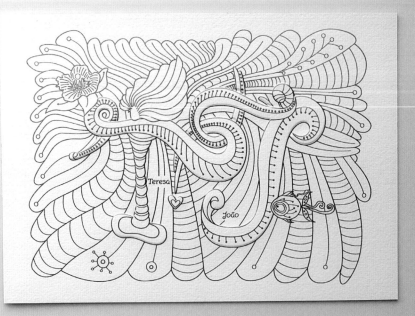

Maria Isabel Marques da Gama
Luís de Mello Pereira Coutinho

&

Maria da Conceição Varela da Silveira e Castro
José Pedro Sant'Anna Medeiros

Têm o prazer de convidar
para o casamento dos seus filhos

Teresa & João

que se realiza na Igreja
da Nossa Senhora da Saúde,
na Quinta da Penha Longa,
em Sintra, no dia 2 de Setembro,
pelas 18h.

RSFF

Teresa                          João                          Rua Mouzinho de Albuquerque
919 459 972                    918 303 976                   n.º 3 - Bloco B, 1º Andar
teresapcoutinho@hotmail.com    jmmedeiros@gmail.com          2765-258 Estoril

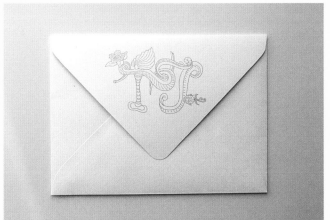

Wedding invitation for a Portuguese couple,
Teresa and João, designed with a simple
embossed illustration.

Kubrick is a fashion brand from Japan, named like this because of the famous American film director, Stanley Kubrick. Studio NewWork created these invitations for the autumn/winter 2012 collection show and spring/summer 2013, and they were based on the color palette of each collection.

131

## EDIBLE SCHOOLYARD SPRING BENEFIT
D: Red Antler
C: Edible Schoolyard New York

Red Antler designed the invitation for the Spring Benefit gala collateral for a nonprofit that partners with New York public schools to build gardens, kitchen classrooms, and opportunity. The Spring Gala is Edible Schoolyard's main method of fundraising so it needed to be incredible. Over a dozen of new york's most acclaimed chefs treated tables to a one-of-a-kind evening. They created the save the date, invites, signage, programs, and menus, making sure that all aspects of this star-studded event were unforgettable. Illustrations of plants and vegetables growing amongst bricks emphasize the organization's close connection to New York City and plans to expand its impact in Harlem.

Invitation for Lydia Delgado's fashion
show. A "Warholian" treatment of femi-
ninity representing the perfume bottle
is underscored by a vibrant color
palette over a heavyweight support
to achieve a flashy, noticeable and
elegant effect.

134

SIMONE & RAMÓN'S WEDDING
D: Neil Cutler
C: S.Scholtz + R.Rodriguez
Invitation for Simone Scholtz and
Ramón Rodríguez wedding. Designed
with a simple and effective message:
Simone says yes! (Sí!) to Ramón.

Si!

Simo!

Simone & Ramón

...zullen gaan trouwen op 12 juni 2003 in Barcelona en je bent/julie zijn van harte uitgenodigd om dit samen met ons te vieren
...celebrarán su boda el día 12 de junio 2003 en Barcelona y estaríamos encantados de contar con tu/vuestra presencia
...are getting married on the 12th of June 2003 in Barcelona and we'd love you to come and celebrate this day with us

CRISTIAN & NATALIA INVITE
D: Sonsoles Llorens
C: Private Client

The King and Queen of Hearts symbolize the couple who marries. The wedding invitations were designed like poker playing cards to provide a lively and playful atmosphere.

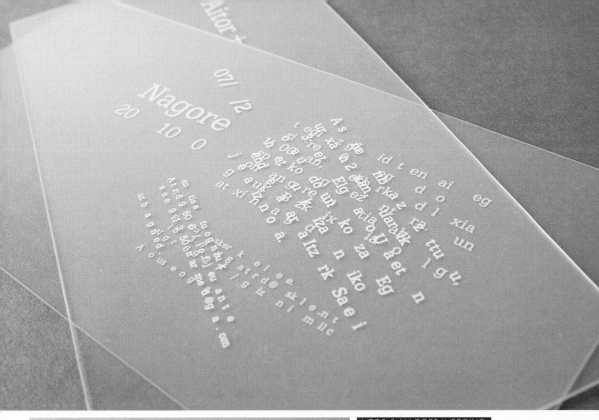

## AITOR & NAGORE WEDDING
### D: La Caja de Tipos
### C: Private Client

According to the RAE (Spanish Language Academy) a wedding is a ceremony in which two people are united in marriage and where both parts are indispensable in order to carry it out. When the designers met with Aitor and Nagore to talk about the invitation they were going to design for them, they commented that this concept seemed very important and that it must be present because in some way it is the essence of the event. They decided that for a project with so much meaning they had to take risks and use a different material: a clear acetate divided in two pieces. Each piece contains one part of the text of the invitation. To emphasize even more this concept of unity they separated the text by letters scattered randomly on both acetates, this way the only way to read fully the text was to bring together these two parts.

**cristina + juanan**

Nos complace invitaros a la ceremonia de enlace que celebraremos el 9 de octubre de 2010 a las 13 del mediodía en la iglesia de San Juan Bautista de Muskiz*.

Comida: Hostal Arenillas (Islares).

Atseginez gonbidatzen zaituztegu. Urriaren 9an, eguerdiko 13etan, Muskizko San Juan Bataiatzaile parrokian ospatuko dugun ezkontza ekizkizunera. Egun honetan gurekin izatea nahiko genuke*.

Bazkaria: Hostal Arenillas (Islares)

Se ruega confirmación.
Erantzutea eskertuko genizuke

**chema + marga**
09/10/2010

**marisa + valen**

CHEMA & MARGA INVITATION
D: LaCaja de Tipos
C: Private Client

The concept idea for this project was to do something different inspired by a traditional wedding habit: the rice shower that guests throw over the newly married couple. When the couple emerges from the ceremony venue, guests toss handfuls of the rice in the air so it showers down over the couple. A plastic bag kit was designed which contained the invitation and a handful of rice ready to be thrown.

## BAAL INVITATION
D: Mamastudio
C: Warsaw New Year's Eve Ball

Mamastudio were invited to participate in
the organization of a New Year's Eve ball
event in a newly opened club in Warsaw. It
was a slightly dark and decadent party with
formal attire and a big band. They decided
that the concept of the celebration would
be Baal—a demon of the Ugaritic mythology.
Each participant received an elegant invitation printed with copper silkscreen and
embossing and a black mask in a sealed
envelope.

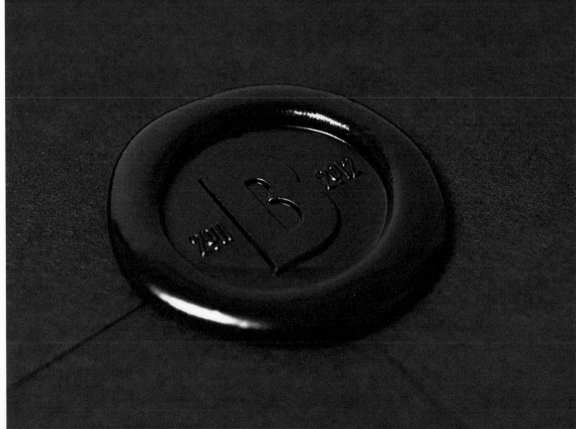

Esther and Kiko got married and five months later they decided to celebrate a wedding party with their family and friends. They wanted to reflert on the invitation their own personalities, so the designers used bright colors and some funny photos made on the court the day of their wedding. Thet also designed and special handmade envelope, as the size of the card was a bit unconventional and a personalized stamp.

Érase una vez

## una boda

DONDE LOS NOVIOS

### SE CASARON

Y CINCO
## MESES
## DESPUÉS...

lo celebraron!

Ya nos dimos
el sí quiero,

ahora toca
**DISFRUTARLO**

Os esperamos el 15 de septiembre
a las 21:00h en Boluda Zaragoza,
Edificio Agustín Florial - Avda. Ranillas, s/n

Kiko &
Esther
15/09/2012

BANTIERRA (Oficina Caja Rural) · 2191 0194 16 5096467

## PORTRAITS INVITATION
D: Kanella
C: Private Client

When life brings people together, it leads them to weave their story as one. A piece of string embraces the invitation and profile portraits were added on top, visualizing the concept. The invitation was created using book-binding cardboard and printed in one-colour letterpress technique.

PASSAVAMO SULLA TERRA LEGGERI
D: Paolo Bazzani
C: Antonio Marras
Invitation for Antonio Marras fashion show
made of lead and engraved with the information of the event. This material allows
to crumple it as a piece of paper.

## TOP SECRET
**D: Kanella**
**C: Private Client**

The concept behind this wedding invitation was based on the fact that nobody, besides the couple, could imagine that they have decided to get married. The tiny wooden box looks like a shipping crate and surprises the recipient with its content. The "top secret" is partially revealed when the guest opens the package and reads the card saying: "See you in September."

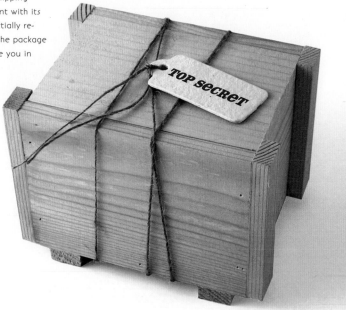

For a baby-boy christening ceremony in
the city of Elassona, Greece, small linen
pouches, in brown and light blue color,
were created as baptism giveaway gifts.
These pouches contained traditional
greek sweets and they were decorated
with small badges with different slogans
and colors. All images are from photographer Michalis Kloukinas.

CERIMONIA DI INAUGURAZIONE
D: Francesca Perani
C: Honegger Health Facility Center
Invitation designed for the commem-
oration of Doctor Maurizio Perani. The
defragmentation of the image through
infinite series of lines produces the effect
of an everlasting memory of the lost one.

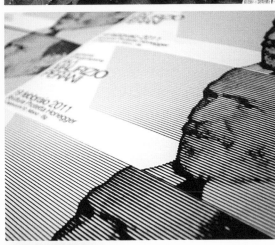

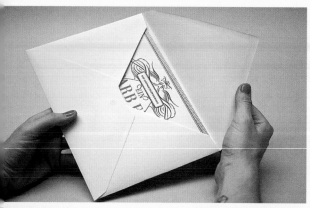

The annual Global Trend Book theme in 2012 was "Wide Awake. Since the Color Show 2012 took place in a theater, the design concept around William Shakespeare's "A Midsummer Night's Dream" was developed and a color "daydream" was created. The Color Show itself was presented on the stage as a play, devided in different acts, so the clients were invited as VIP premiere guests. Based on this concept invitations, programs and the book were designed.
To reflect the classiness of the invitation of this event the printing technique of letterpress was chosen, rounded down with high class paper and beautiful typographic illustrations.

V. ARTURO SOLARTE SOLARTE
R. STELLA G. DE SOLARTE

~ Participan el enlace de sus hijos ~

## NORA PATRICIA

Y tienen el gusto de invitarle
a la ceremonia religiosa que se celebrará
el viernes tres de Agosto de dos mil doce,
a las seis y treinta de la tarde,
en la Iglesia del Convento de Santo Domingo
de Cartagena, Colombia.

BOGOTÁ Y STÄFA, JUNIO DE DOS MIL DOCE

PETER E. SCHULTHESS
MERET SCHULTHESS

~ Teilen ihnen die Vermählung ihrer Kinder ~

## GIAN DIMITRI

mit und haben die Ehre
Sie zur kirchlichen Trauung
am Freitag, 3. August 2012, 18.30 Uhr,
in die Iglesia del Convento
de Santo Domingo, Cartagena de India,
Kolumbien, einzuladen.

BOGOTÁ UND STÄFA, IM JUNI 2012

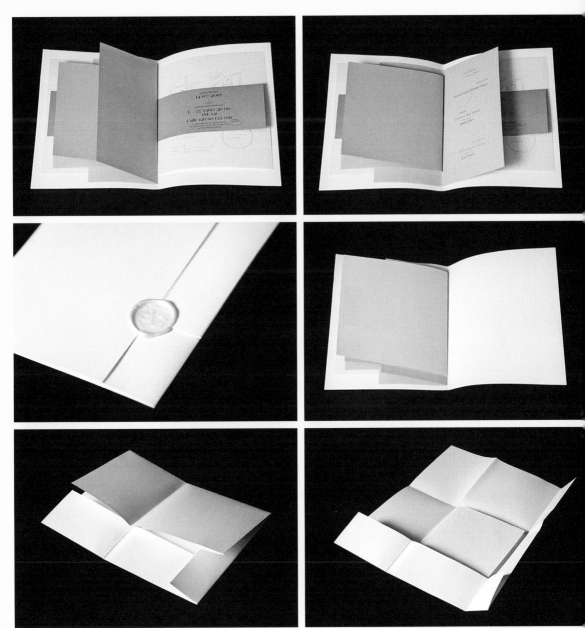

## NORA PATRICIA & GIAN INVITATION
D: Raquel Quevedo
C: Patricia Solarte

Wedding invitation designed for Nora Patricia, from Colombia, and Giant from Zurich. The invitation was created using couple's original languages: Spanish and German. This way both family guests can choose their respective language to read the invitation.

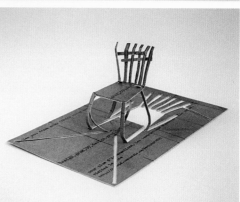

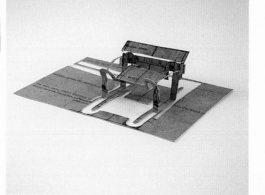

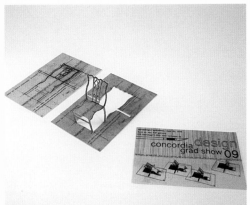

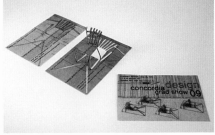

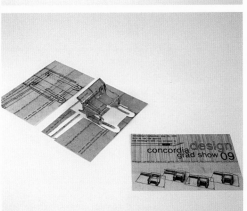

CU DESIGN GRAD SHOW PROMS
D: Derek Broad
C: Concordia University

Winning submission in the promotional package competition for the Concordia University 2009 Design Graduation Show. The promotions included a collection of interactive invitations and a catalogue that explore the possibilities of pop-up and the interaction between 2-D and 3-D design. Invitations featured a series of three designer chair pop-ups: Marcel Breuer's Wesley chair, Frank Gehry's Hat-Trick chair and a Thomas Chippendale-style ribbon back chair. Those receiving the invitation could follow a simple guide to cut, fold and create their own 3-D chair.

MARTINI TERRAZZA
D: Musa Work Lab
C: Martini, Dolce & Gabbana

Invitation for Martini and Dolce & Gabbana's Gold
launch in Portugal, designed in two spot color–
black and gold pantone–printed on high gloss
paper with gold hot stamping, embossed finishings
and folded to keep the main invitation inside.

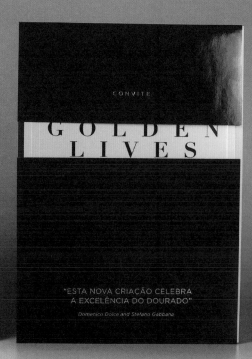

The Spanish

# OPEN

28th April-1st May 2000

The European

# OPEN

Hamburg 18th-21st May 2000

The US

# OPEN

15th-18th June 2000

The British

# OPEN

20th-23rd July 2000

The Italian

# OPEN

26th-29th October 2000

The Westin La Quinta Golf Resort, Marbella

# OPENING

3rd November 2000

OPENING WESTIN LA QUINTA GOLF RESORT
D: Neil Cutler
C: Inversiones Hoteleras La Quinta
Invitation to the grand opening of the golf resort hotel The Westin La Quinta in Marbella, Spain. Play on words using the dates of the major golf events of the year: The British Open, The US Open, etc.

## ISOLA MARRAS INVITATION
D: Paolo Bazzani
C: Antonio Marras

The autumn/winter 2013 collection from Italian fashion brand Isola Marras was inspired by the Nordic sea during the winter season, and by Virginia Woolf's novel *To The Lighthouse*. The invitation was designed as a pop-up lighthouse and during the runway the models appeared inside a boat on a sea made of blue painted books.

ESTORIL FASHION ART FESTIVAL
D: Musa Work Lab
C: Estoril Fashion Art

Assorted invitations for Estoril Fashion
Art Festival 1st Edition. Different printing
techniques over different papers and
cardboard.

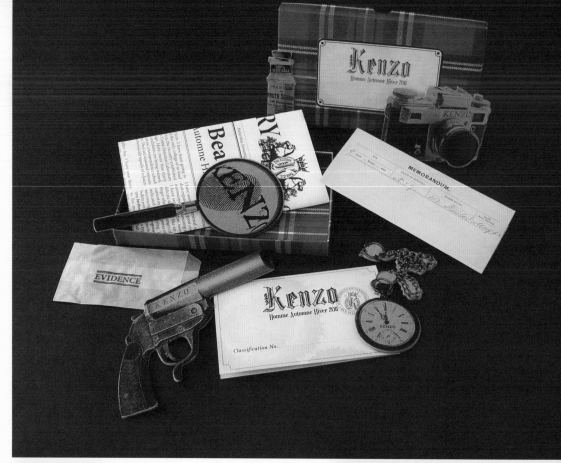

KENZO SHERLOCK
D: Paolo Bazzani
C: Kenzo

This invitation for Kenzo's fashion show
was a small tartan box containing a kit
with everything a detective could need
for his or her investigations. Sherlock
Holmes was the clear inspiration for the
collection.

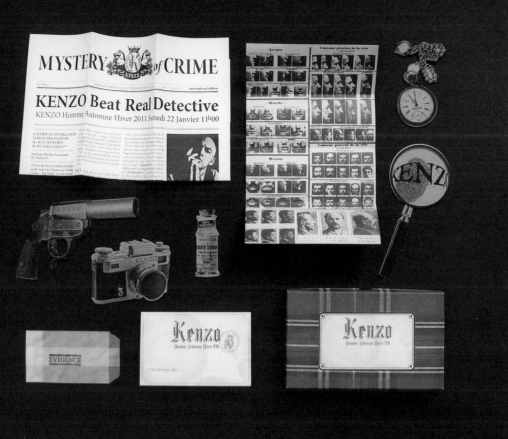

## 50 GREATEST HITS
**D:** Is Creative Studio
**C:** Lucy Pardo & Carlos Lopez

Lucy and Carlos are music lovers. This couple has a great collection of music from the 40s, 50s, and 60s, and many of their lives shared moments are associated to a song. The invitation for their golden wedding must have to describe their personality. The studio designed a sleeve and stickers for real 7-inch vinyls bought on an antique shop with random tracks, an invitation to enjoy surprise and discover new music. Every year has been a succesful aniversary of marriage, like a greatest hit.

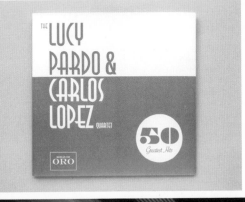

The concept of this wedding derives from the particularity of the celebrated day—the four names celebrated on this day could very well be wishes for the couple, for a happy marriage. It has to be noted that in Greece name days takes great importance, similar to birthdays. The invitation was created in four versions. In the front side we can see the text with the necessary instructions for the ceremony, and on the back side four different illustrations were created, dedicated to each of the wishes with accompanying texts explaining the meaning of each one. The style and the illustrations of the invitations are based on well-known symbolism. For the guests giveaway packages, paper small boxes were created with the same illustration themes containing sugared almonds.

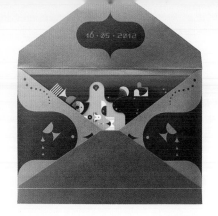

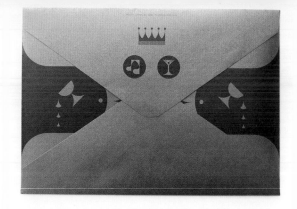

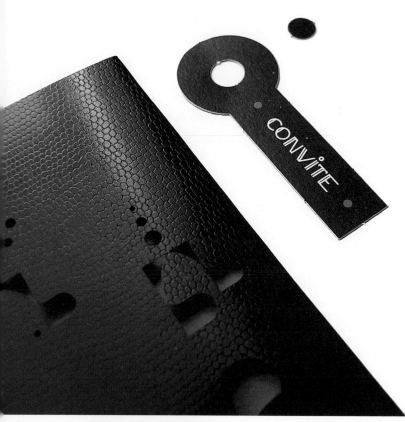

In May 2012 reopened doors a mythical concert hall of Lisbon, Portugal, the Ritz Clube. The three partners of this new administration contacted Maga Studio to project the identity and communication. After reviewing the extensive history and the architectural richness of the building, the clear objective was to reinterpret the language par excellence of the 20s and 30s decorative arts: The Art Deco. Together with the client, they wanted to embrace and honour its history but also wanted a new and modern Ritz Club. The whole language, which is born from the reinterpretation of Deco forms and their demultiplication, was designed to meet this objective.

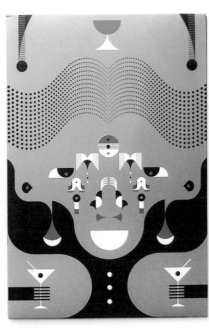

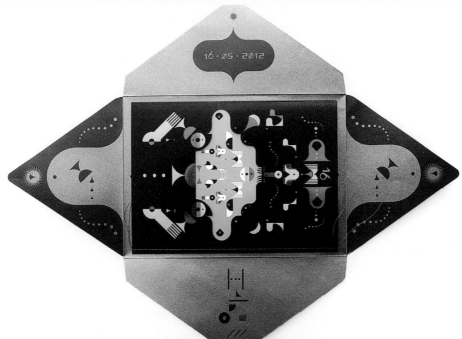

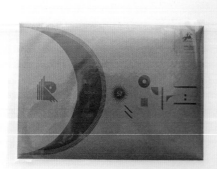

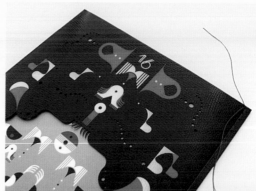

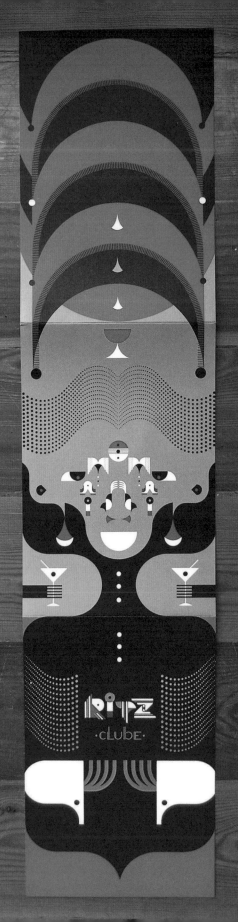

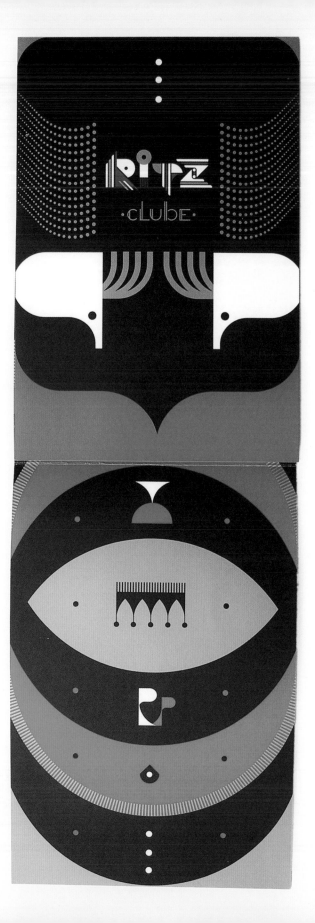

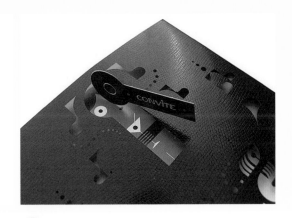

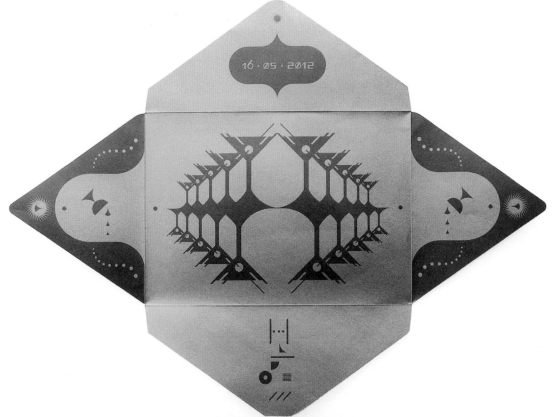

TAST DE VINS
D: Anna Jordà
C: Private Client

The invitation is a glued diptych designed
for a group of wine lovers that organize
wine tastings and in which participates both
professional and amateur winemakers. Three
icons have been created as a brand from
the three basic steps to start a wine tasting:
sight, smell and taste.

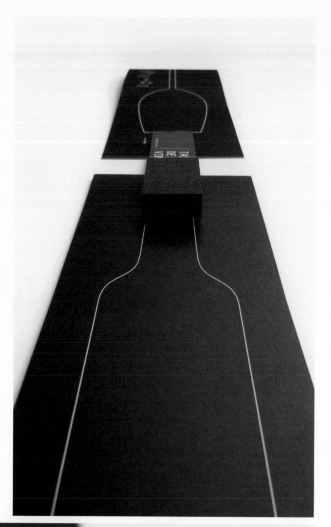

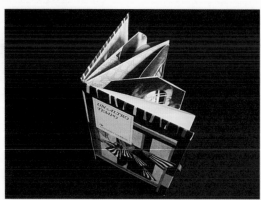

## UN ALTRO TEMPO
### D: Paolo Bazzani
### C: Antonio Marras

Antonio Marras autumn/winter 20013-2014
show was dedicated to the Bloomsbury
group, an historical group of british
artists, writers, poets and designers such
as Virginia Woolf, Vita Sackerville-West
and Ezra Pound. The invitation wanted
to recreate the house in which they used
to gather and create. The outside is a
typical british book, and when you open it
becomes a four-rooms house pop-up. Each
room is made with pictures of the British
group members.

TIKOU TIKOU
D: Despina Aeraki
C: Private Client

During her meeting with Katrina's mom
and dad, Despina tried to discover the
most cute details of this little baby-girl
personality. She picked up "tikou-tikou,"
out of her babytalk, to illustrate this
invitation. She also drew a bear on it,
because a bear-doll was her favorite toy.
The fabric bib-invitations were offered as
wrapped presents to the guests.

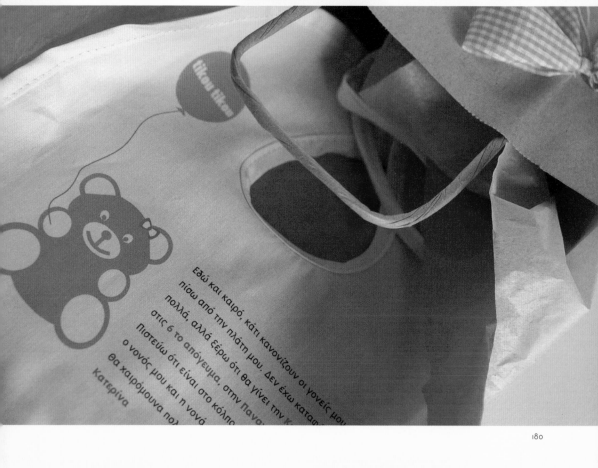

Εδώ και καιρό, κάτι κανονίζουν οι γονείς μου
πίσω από την πλάτη μου. Δεν έχω καταλ
πολλά, αλλά ξέρω ότι θα γίνει την Κ
στις 6 το απόγευμα, στην Πανα
Πιστεύω ότι είναι στο κόλπο
ο νονός μου και η νονά
θα χαιρόμουνα πο
Κατερίνα

Donica Ida designed these save the dates
for a travel-themed wedding in Hawaii.

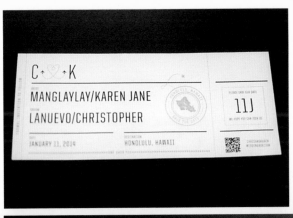

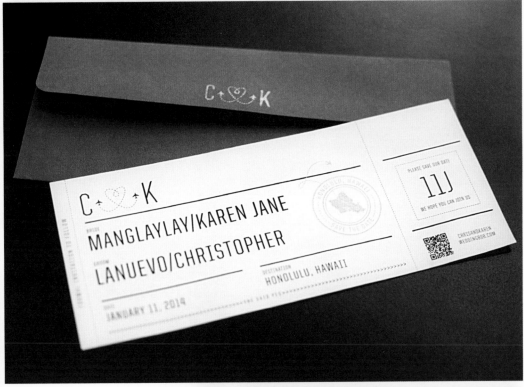

Carlos Guerreiro from Maga designed this opening invitation
for Babel, a new Fabrico Infinito concept shop and gallery
space in Lisbon, Portugal.

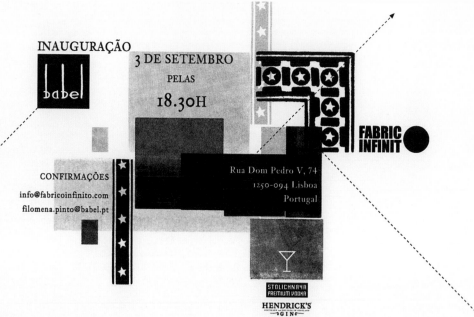

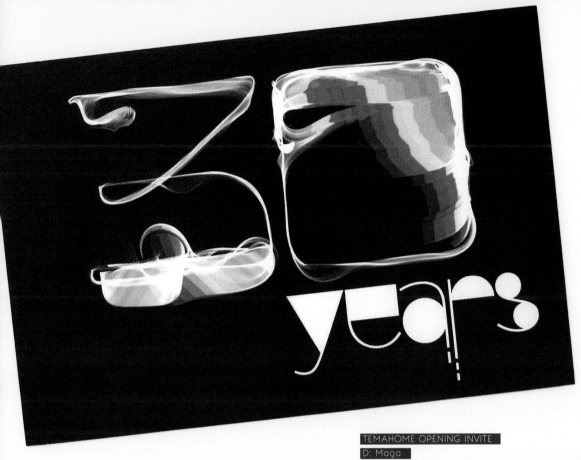

TEMAHOME OPENING INVITE
D: Maga
C: Temahome

30th anniversary's party Invitation for furniture design brand TemaHome.

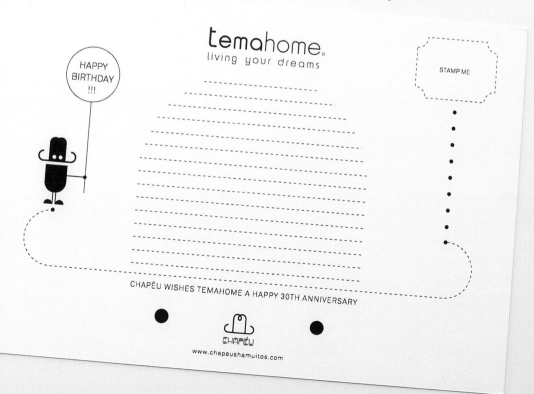

**temahome**.
living your dreams

HAPPY
BIRTHDAY
!!!

STAMP ME

---------------------------

------------------------------

-----------------------------

-----------------------------

-----------------------------

-----------------------------

-----------------------------

-----------------------------

-----------------------------

-----------------------------

-----------------------------

-----------------------------

CHAPÉU WISHES TEMAHOME A HAPPY 30TH ANNIVERSARY

CHAPÉU
www.chapeushamuitos.com

Because of professional meanings, Laia and Carles began their married life living in different cities: Barcelona and Pekin. Their immediate future were full of comings and goings between both cities, starting with Carles first trip to Barcelona to celebrate their wedding party. In the next months the aircraft would be their umbilical cord. The couple wanted to reflect this situation on their wedding invitation so the design was inspired by a flight ticket and other stuff such as boarding passes or luggage tag labels with the name of the guests.

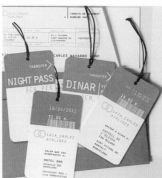

NeonNiche studio were asked to create a unique invite for a black and white themed music awards night. The Musik Awards invitation is a concertina fold invite enclosed in a bespoke velvet envelope. Upon opening the invite a pop up chair is revealed to the recipient, showing them the seat reserved for them for the award night. Innovative design paired with a deep understanding of the clients needs resulted in a product well received by the client and the invitees.

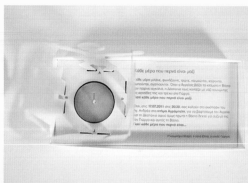

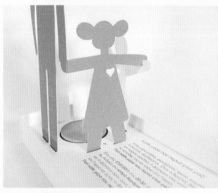

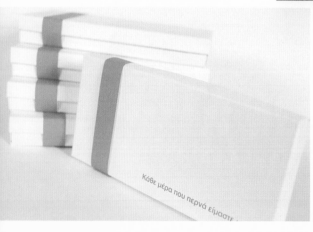

Giorgos and Vassia were about to get married and christen both of their children, Angelos and Despina, at the same time. Designing a common invitation for the three ceremonies was a major creative challenge. A candle was the key object of the invitation, considering its flame as the flame of love. The precut family figures were to be attached at the notches around the candle and its light was supposed to pass through the heart-shaped windows of each figure. The invitation box also contained an instruction manual for putting the pieces together properly, as well as a red heart-shaped sticker for the guests wishes. The favor was a paper-cut baby cube with the first four letters of the Greek alphabet, which also happen to be the name initials of the family members and the gift was a red heart with the family figures, made of plexiglass. Special paper horns were printed for the wedding ceremony and paper hearts were mixed into their rice filling; a special a special frame also created, allowing the guests to stick the invitation hearts with their wishes on it. The project was developed as an interactive game, starting the moment that the guest would open the invitation box and ending when he would stick his own wishes heart on the wishes frame.

1. HAZLE CASO A TU CO
3. APRENDE A PERDONAR
APOYO 7. DALE SUS GUST
SIEMPRE TENDRÁS LA RAZ
LIENZO, UNA OBRA MAEST
REALIDAD 15. ESFORZÁND
QUE LE GUSTE 18. TOMEN
MOMENTOS QUE PASAN J
EL AMOR Y ALIMÉNTENLO
26. COMPARTAN SUS VA
MAÑANAS CON MUCHO
PELEAS SON LAS RECON
SIEMPRE SERÁ LO MÁS IN
TAMBIÉN ES UNA OPCIÓN
ALGUNA VEZ 39. LOS HALA
ES LA CLAVE 42. NUNCA
44. ANTES DE EMPEZAR U
SE PASAN EN FAMILIA 4
49. EN LO QUE NO PUEDA

AÑOS

**CARLOS Y LAURA**

50 TIPS
D: Is Creative Studio
C: Laura Ruiz + Carlos Meza

Carlos Meza and Laura Ruiz have many stories to share, a very kind couple that are always willing to help someone in need. They request an invitation for their 50th wedding anniversary something precious that guests want to keep. Achieving 50 years of marriage is a heroic deed. The studio asked Carlos and Laura to write 50 advices to have a long and happy relationship to placed them in the invitation as a gift to the guests of the ceremony.

Campaign raising awareness in the recognition of the city as the
birthplace of painter Giambattista Moroni, one of the most famous North Italian portrait specialists of the 16th century–whose
work is exhibited at the National Gallery of London. The design
is the result of a combination of contemporary fonts, geometric
textureand hand-written reminiscent of the historical period in
which the painter lived.

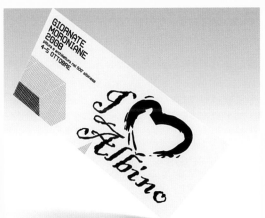

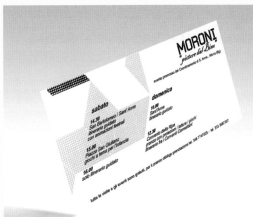

ANTONIO MARRAS NIVOLA
D: Paolo Bazzani
C: Antonio Marras

Dedicated to the sardinian artist Costantino
Nivola, it was delivered to guest a carboard box
containing soil inside a printed napkin. On the
napkin it was one of Nivola's poem about sea
and his beloved Sardinia.

Invitation designed for a wedding held in the south of France. The Spanish-French couple decided that the theme for the ceremony should refer to some Spanish traditions. The floral drawing of a "mantilla"–a typical Spanish feminine blanket top used in celebrations and major events–was used as the main design element. Another items used were the fan and the carnations–characteristic southern Spain flowers. Real fans and carnations were also distributed as a gift to the guests.

NAT & PAUL'S WEDDING
D: Amanda Alessi
C: Private Client

The brief was to create a wedding stationery set that included an invitation, gift registry, accommodation and RSVP card. The wedding stationery set was designed to reflect the traditional styling and structure of Paul and Natalie's wedding. The couple also wanted a subtle peacock theme incorporated into the invitation due to the inclusion of peacock feathers in the bouquets. The overall tone of voice was elegance and romance. The letterpress printing was completed by the fabulous Phil and Ann at Whiteman Park Print Shop in Western Australia.

Getxophoto, a photography festival, asked to the studio to design the poster and invitation for the 6th edition of the event, wich theme was "In Praise of Childhood". To develop the concept they thought about which was the common thing that children of very different ages love to do besides playing, and art-related activity, and that how they find the coloring books. A series of three invitations and posters in collaboration with Guchagucha's studio–formed by the Japanese Michi Roji and the Argentine Eduardo Bertone– that created all the illustrations. Gala, 3 years old, she painted the "Getxophoto in the forest," Isabel 5 years old, she painted "Getxophoto in the city," and Félix, 6 years old, he painted "Getxophoto in space."

# GETXOPHOTO 2012

## UMEEI GORAZARRE / ELOGIO DE LA INFANCIA
Iraila / Septiembre

antolatzailea / organiza    babesleak / patrocinan

 BEGIHANDI     Getxo     BFA DFB     EUSKO JAURLARITZA GOBIERNO VASCO     Estudios Durero    bbk=

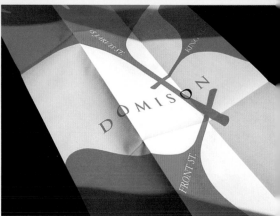

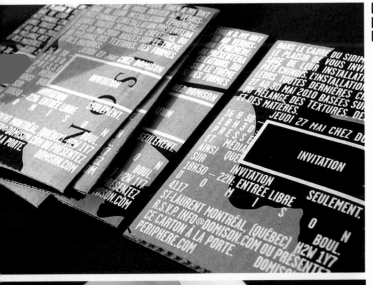

DOMISON INVITATION
D: Paprika
C: Domison

The mandate was to create an invitation
for the opening of the new Domison's
boutique in Toronto, Canada. Paprika
studio made a folding game with that.
On one side, the new boutique address,
on the other side the Domison logo. They
used the emblem of Domison which is a
Ginkgo Biloba leaf as the graphic charter.
Playing with the leafs, they let appear
the city map with the principal city street
names: Jarvis Street, King Street, and
Front Street. To finish, in the middle, the
"o" letter of Domison was a "here" indica-
tion telling were the boutique is located.

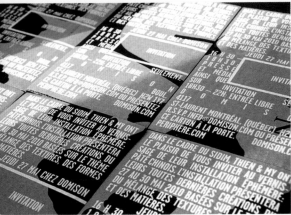

Opening invitation designed by Carlos
Guerreiro at Maga studio for Chapéu in
Lisbon, Portugal.

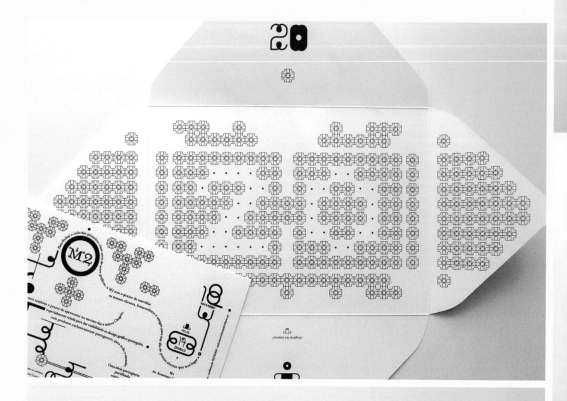

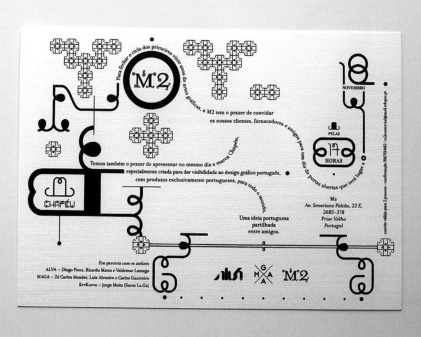

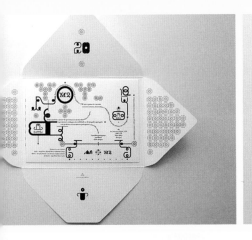

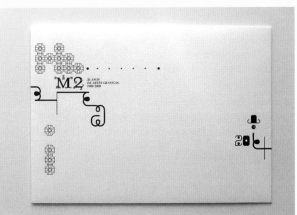

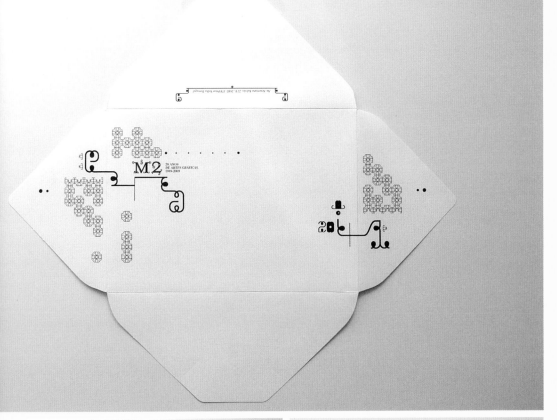

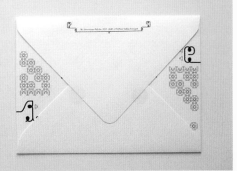

**MYRIAM & ROBERTO**
D: El Calotipo
C: Private Client

Wedding invitation cards for Myriam and Roberto's
wedding. A total print run of 200 copies, helped
the design studio to get the final quality they were
looking for the stamping. The design development
was not complicated, as soon as they presented
the first sketch to their clients they loved it so
much and they didn't want to change anything.
The hardest part was to get a clean letterpress
printing without ink coming out of the footprint.
The whole invitation–except for the forefront–was
produced using photopolymer printed with a FAG
Control 405 letterpress proof press.

Podi, the food orchard, is a new all day restaurant that celebrates bold, robust and unique flavours. Podi is the brainchild of Cedele and upholds Cedele's philosophy of advocating buying and making food deliciously, and most importantly, responsibly. Derived from the meaning of Podi in Hindi–a corse mixture of ground dry spices and herbs–a simple and modern logo mark with strong colour accents was developed, drawing inspiration from heaped spoonfuls of various spices and herbs mounds. The earthy tones used throughout in color palette to imagery is applied to reflect Podi's mission of making good, natural and organic food.

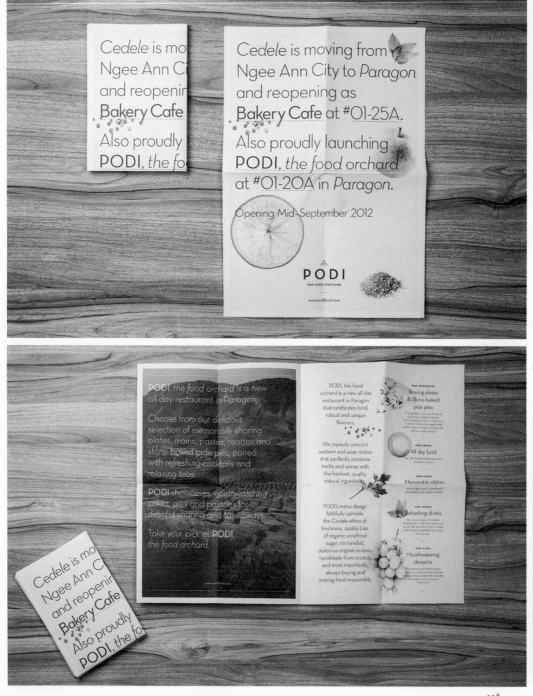

208

PODI, the food orchard is a new all day restaurant in Paragon, that celebrates bold, robust and unique flavours.

We joyously concoct western and asian dishes that perfectly combine herbs and spices with the freshest, quality natural ingredients.

PODI's menu design faithfully upholds the Cedele ethos of freshness, quality (use of organic unrefined sugar, no transfat), delicious original recipes,

PODI
THE FOOD ORCHARD
www.podifood.com

PODI LOVES
Memorable dishes
We lovingly create a selection of memorable mains, pastas, risottos

PODI BLENDS
Refreshing drinks
We serve a range of cocktails blended with fresh fruits, herbs and spices. We also offer made-to-order fresh fruit and vegetable juices, and relaxing teas.

PODI BAKES
Mouthwatering
desserts

Cedele is moving from Ngee Ann City to Paragon and reopening as Bakery Cafe. Also proudly PODI, the foo

Cedele is moving from Ngee Ann City to Paragon and reopening as Bakery Cafe at #01-25A.

Also proudly launching PODI, the food orchard at #01-20A in Paragon.

Opening Mid-September 2012

Choose a selection of plates, mains, stone-baked pi with refreshing coo relaxing teas.

PODI showcases mouth cakes, pies and pastries dessert sharing and Take your pi the food o

D & K WEDDING INVITATION
D: Bureau Rabensteiner
C: Klaus Ehrenfried

"Shabby chic with a squeeze of lemon."
This is the stationary and invitation
design for a beautiful wedding on
Mallorca, Spain.

MODA LISBOA FASHION FORCE
D: Musa Work Lab
C: Moda Lisboa

Assorted invitation designs for ModaLisboa's 33th edition, this time tittled "Fashion Force."

Invitation for Lydia Delgado spring/summer 2009 fashion show presentation.
A very contrasted collage that gives a modern, fresh and contemporary design.

By Invite Only is a handcrafted jewellery
brand with a rustic art direction. Bravo
Company decided to give it a vintage
circus look using old photographies and
choosing a typography that remind us to
the early 20th century carnival tickets.

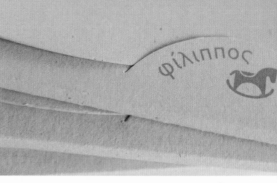

φίλιππος

Filippos is a really pretty baby and his photo would certainly make a beautiful invitation. After a long photo shooting, Despina, the designer, chose the best picture along with the parents and then she decided to print it on a thick cardboard that was cut into pieces, in order to create a puzzle. The invitation was enclosed into a specially designed envelope.

ANDER & MARÍA

FER & NORA WEDDING INVITE
D: La Caja de Tipos
C: Fer Ansola + Nora Formariz

Fer and Nora wanted all their guests to participate actively the day of their wedding, to make it a day to remember. The studio designed the invitation in two parts, one with the event data and how-to instructions, and the other one with a series of small laser-cut perforated circles that can be separated. This way guests can play with it giving different wedding element shapes to their invitations. The instructions gave ideas, but everyone was free to do what they want to get a personal touch to their own invitation. Then the leftover circles become confetti to be thrown to the newlyweds when they leave the church, helping to create a party atmosphere from the very first minute.

FER & NORA

Tenemos el gusto de invitaros a nuestra boda el próximo día 19 de marzo a las 12:30 horas en la iglesia Santa María de Deba. Para celebrarlo todos juntos, a continuación ofreceremos un cóctel de bienvenida seguido del banquete en el restaurante Otzarreta de Zarautz.

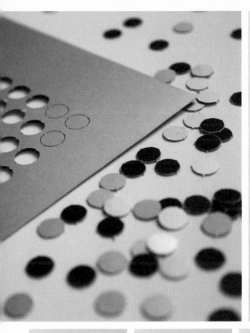

FER & NORA
FER & NORA
FER & NORA
FER & NORA
FER & NORA

# FER & NORA

Invitation designed for BASF Coatings GmbH Color Show. For this event the special theme was "Come Closer Club"—a fictional private Club for honorary members. In this familial atmosphere the members had the great pleasure to see and know the recently developed Special Collection of Color Coatings. Based on this concept invitations and additional event accessories were designed. Together with the invitation every member received a Club Box with different sized vessels and was requested to collect favorite items with great color impressions to show and discuss later at the workshop.

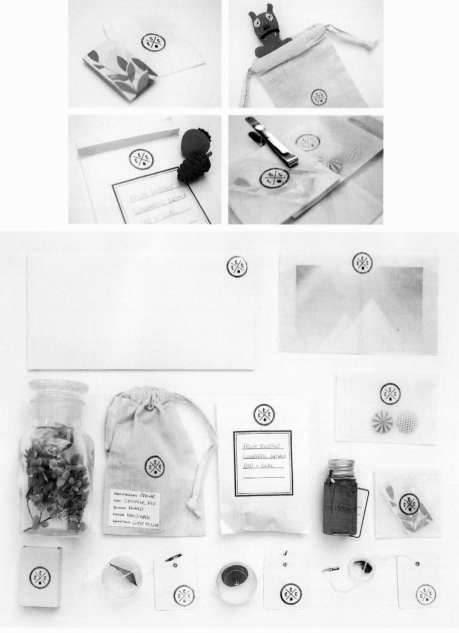

The Stewart Foundation asked Paprika to design a printed item commemorating the 30th anniversary of the Liliane and David M. Stewart Collection. This item was to be a souvenir for guests at three events to celebrate the anniversary in Montreal, New York and Paris, and featuring the launch of a book, The Century of Modern Design: Selections from the Liliane and David M. Stewart Collection. The inspiration was based in all the events organized by the Liliane and David M. Stewart Foundation in the past 30 years. The poster that we designed is divided into 33 equal sections, each having the dimensions and appearance of a ticket to an art exhibit: one section for each year, and three final sections containing further information about the Foundation. A list of all the events, with historical details, appears on the back of the poster.

Invitation designed for the Dom Pérignon by Marc
Newson launch into the Portuguese market. The
invitations were printed over a saville row dark gray
paper with blind emboss and hot stamping.

The Antonio Marras collection was dedicated to Henry Darger and some of the traditional british celebrations. The invitation was a small box with Wedwood-like engravings containig a rounded biscuit with a sugar cameo on. The setting of the runway show was a british banquet, with rounded tables from were the guest could watch the show and enjoy tea, coffee and biscuits served at the same time.

## KIT DE SUPERVIVENCIA DEL INVITADO
**D: Binocular Studio**
**C: Sheila + Sam**

Binocular Studio designed this amusing "Guest's Survival Kit" containing, in addition to the invitation, all the essentials to have fun during a wedding: a handkerchief for those who cannot hold back the tears, a band-aid for guests with new shoes, some rice to throw to the couple, and a "Bride Friends" badge.

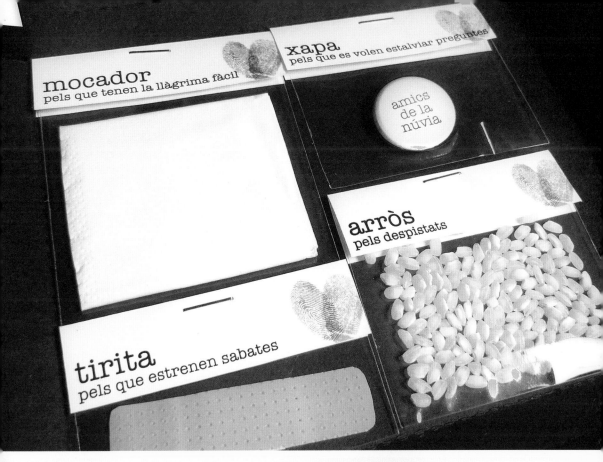

mocador
pels que tenen la llàgrima fàcil

xapa
pels que es volen estalviar preguntes

amics
de la
núvia

arròs
pels despistats

tirita
pels que estrenen sabates

sheila+samuel

kit de
supervivència
del convidat
IMPRESCINDIBLES D'EMERGÈNCIA

Invitation design for Weber Shandwick's
10th anniversary party. Foiled on GF Smith
Colorplan Pristine White and Ebony and
supplied with matching Ebony envelopes.
Printed by Generation Press.

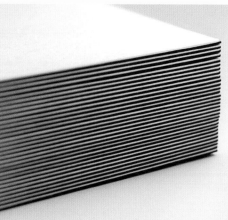

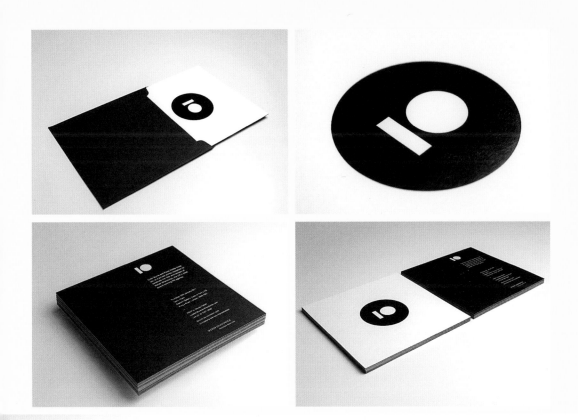

Colin Byrne and Fiona Noble invite you to a private drinks reception to celebrate the 10th anniversary of Weber Shandwick, the UK's most award-winning PR agency.

Thursday 20th January 2011

KATO
plechtige communie

KATO VAN DEN STEEN plechtige communie 18 April 2010

## KATO & PELLE PARTY INVITATION
### D: The Tiny Red Factory
### C: Private Client

Collection of ten images created for a children's party invitations celebrating their love for fantastical story's. The parents request was to create something to keep and remember this occasion. All invited friends got a set of five prints held together by a lightweight paper wrap in their favorite color.

... πριν από ενάμιση περίπου χρόνο
η μαμά μου και ο μπαμπάς μου
ήθελαν να δουν πως θα είναι ένα
μισό Νάσος και μισό Γιώτα!

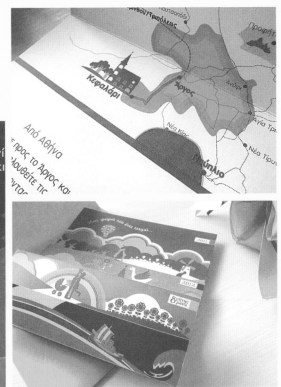

This is a lovely and sweet invitation for the baptism of a beautiful girl, Maria Elena. Her parents hired Untill Sunday to design an invitation that shows how the nine month's long trip started. They thought that it would be nice for their baby-girl, once she's grown up, to know how much they wanted her and cared about her. The invitation was folded into four parts, each one refering to a specific moment of the story: the birth, the journey of pregnancy, the eight months later, and the baptism. On the back side, there is an illustration of the map and the address to the church. With the help of Google Maps, they also added a link in which guests could also see the place online. Also a nice pinwheel was designed and distributed to all guests as a souvenir of this beautiful and happy day. The invitation was printed in four colours on matt paper. The pinwheel was printed in two colours on a matt paper.

JUCO FASHION INVITATIONS
D: Usaginensen
C: Juco shoes

Assorted fashion show invitations designed for Juco, a shoes
creator based in Tokyo, Japan.

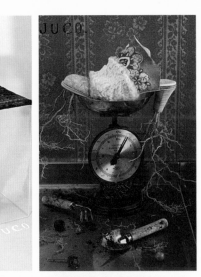

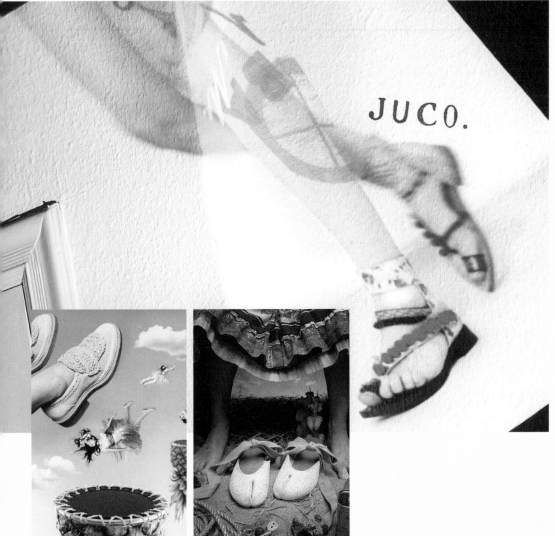

spectacular architecture
& comunication
via cappuccini 3 / 24021 Albino
Italy        ////////////
info@spectacularch.com /
spectacularch.com    ////

SpectaculArch!

Francesca Perani Sandra Marchesi architetti associati

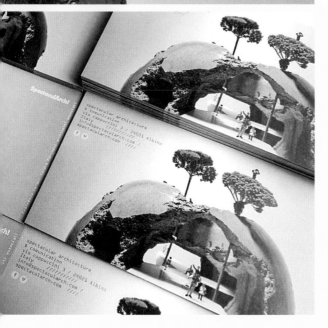

A PLANET FOR THE RESEARCH
D: Francesca Perani
C: Spectacularch!

Invitations designed for the exhibition A planet for the Research, 22 architects in support of Foundation A.R.M.O.R. held at Gallery of Modern and Contemporary Art in Bergamo, Italy.

Fernanda Porto designed this amusing invitation for the Creative Method Christmas Party titled "Nightmare Before Christmas." The designer slayer kit was given to all guests featuring a selection of items to ward themselves from evil-creative spirits.

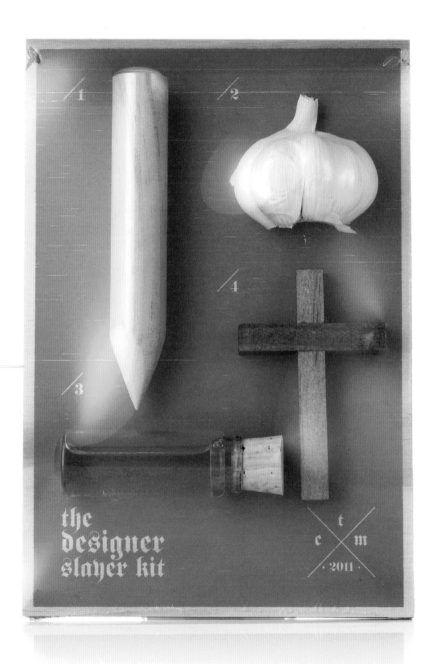

# it's the nightmare before christmas

YOU'RE INVITED TO WALK AMONGST THE DESIGNER DEAD AT OUR
CHRISTMAS EXTRAVAGANZA. WITH KILLER DEADLINES, MURDEROUS BRIEFS
& BUDGET BLUDGEONING AT A GHOULISH END-OF-YEAR HIGH,
IT'S A DO-OR-DIE NIGHT TO CELEBRATE WITH THOSE MOST DEPRAVED
OF OVERWORKED SPIRITS: GRAPHIC DESIGNERS.

---

# the designer slayer kit – your 'how-to' guide

STAVE OFF THESE SADISTIC FALLEN ANGELS WITH THE FOLLOWING
WEAPONS-OF-CHOICE:

| / 1 | / 2 | / 3 | / 4 |
|---|---|---|---|
| **the stake** | **the garlic** | **the holy water** | **the cross** |
| Designers may be hell-bent on revenge for every client change during logo development. GIF it all you've got & go straight for the heart. | Worn around the neck, this kitchen favourite becomes the killer 'in-your-face' ingredient to keeping deadline-crazed designers at bay. | For every angst-ridden, burnt-out designer with Illustrator issues, douse generously for a truly graphic demise. | Have faith! Placed in every moaning designer-type face, this powerful tool will send them straight to the gatefolds of Hell. |

---

**AT THE HOUSE OF TERROR**
*The Creative Method*
*Studio 10, 50 Reservoir Street, Surry Hills*

**BETWEEN THE HAUNTED HOURS**
*7pm – 7am*

**ON THE DARK NIGHT**
*Friday 2 December 2011*

**IN THE DEADLY DRESS CODE**
*Cocktail / Casual / Killer*

---

*Warning: If you want to come out alive, you may wish to bring your kit with you.
It's vital protection against these pantone-possessed paranormals.*

Invitation designed by Paprika studio for
Ramacieri Soligo's cocktail party.

MACIERI SOLIGO
OUS INVITE À UN
COCKTAIL RÉUNISSANT
LES PASSIONNÉS
DE L'ARCHITECTURE
ET DU DESIGN. /
RAMACIERI SOLIGO
IS PLEASED TO INVITE
YOU TO A COCKTAIL
UNITING ARCHITECTURE
AND DESIGN LOVERS.

Présentation /
Showcase :
Nouvelles
New

Collections &
Salle d'exposition
Showroom

Robinetterie /
Faucets
Fantini

Baignoires /
Baths
Bisazza

Carreaux italiens /
Italian tiles
Mutina

RS
VP

à / to :

Avant le jeudi
23 août 2012, en
précisant le nombre
de personnes.

Before Thursday
August 23rd 2012. Please
indicate the number
of attendees.

marketing@
ramacierisoligo.
com

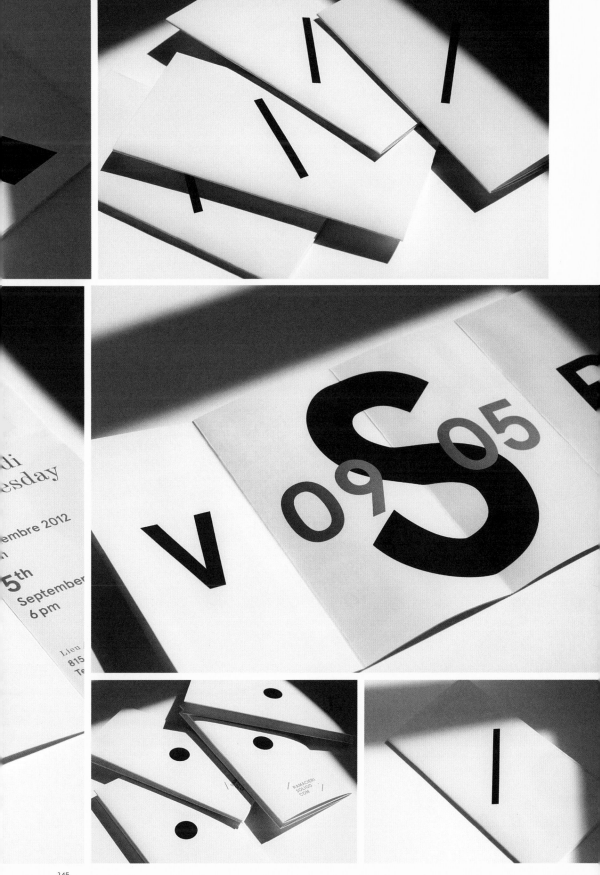

**Burnt Sugar** *invites* **YOU** to **PUT YOUR** **ARTISTIC** skills **IN** the **FRAME** & join **US** in the **DRAWING ROOM** → BOROUGH Market ON the 6th of OCTOBER.

HERE'S

BURNT SUGAR DRAWING ROOM
D: D-Studio
C: Burnt Sugar

Burnt Sugar is a boutique brand of fudge with humble beginnings. This invitation was sent to journalists, food bloggers, industry press, and universities. Inside the brightly coloured envelope, which carried the main invite message, was a postcard explaining the launch of the new branding and a bag to practice doodling on—complete with pen so there were no excuses not to get the creative juices flowing! All was designed by D-Studio and illustrated by Gemma Correll, Jess Wilson, Nick Deakin, Kate Sutton and Rudi de Wet.

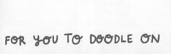

FOR YOU TO DOODLE ON

247

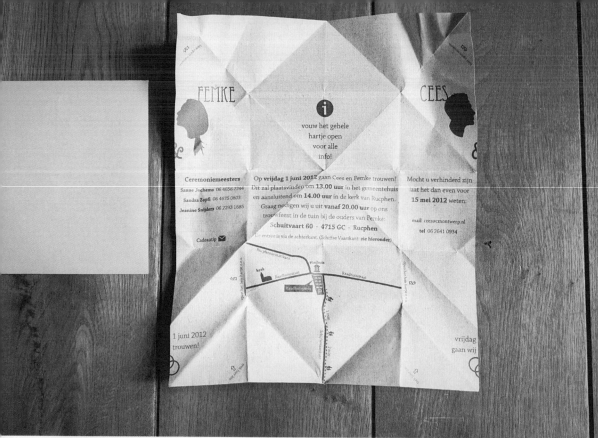

## ORIGAMI WEDDING INVITATION
### D: Cees
### C: Self-Initiated

Wedding invitation designed for the
designer's wedding himself. He created
a heart out of a single paper. If you
unfold the heart the information
comes out. Made with silkscreen and
cardboard paper.

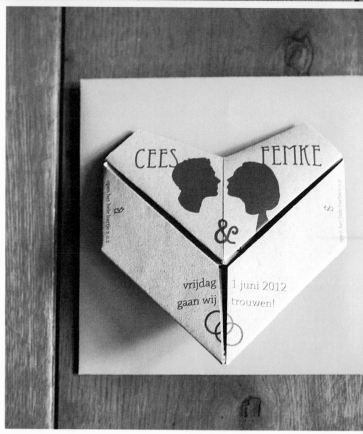

ANTONIO MARRAS FARFALLE
D: Paolo Bazzani
C: Antonio Marras

Inspired by Bright Star movie, the invite
for this Antonio Marras fashsion show
was a small rounded box. As soon as you
open it you'll experience the illusion of
paper butterflies flying out of the box.

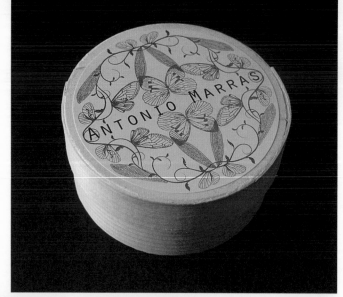

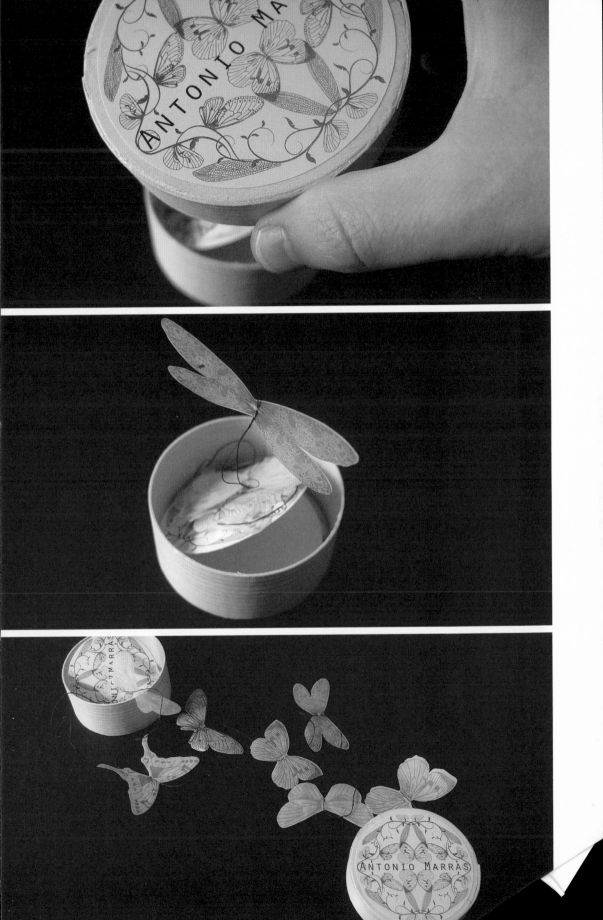

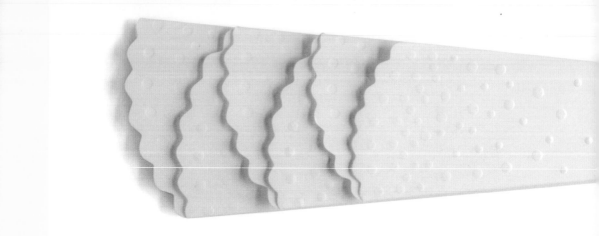

Chiara & James

On the 10th October, 3.30pm in the Taupaki Historic Hall

Please rsvp by 28th August via T 9 810 9899
or email chairajames.wedding@xtra.co.nz

The designer was asked to create a
wedding invite for some of his very close
friends. The brief requested that the invite
marry the bride's wish for "frilly" detail, the
grooms vision for simple, contemporary
styling and the Victorian tea party theme
planned for the wedding. A visit to this
couple's rural property revealed a shared
love of the New Zealand bush and the
native birds that visited their porch, in par-
ticular the Fantail. In fact the Fantail was
an illustrated detail inside the brides dress
and is the feature of the groom's tattoo.

ara & James

er, 3.30pm

253

# CONTRIBUTORS

ÁLVARO VILLARRUBIA
www.alvarovillarrubia.com
P 75.

ALSON LOW
www.behance.net/addiction
P 30.

ANNA JORDÀ
www.annajorda.cat
P 176, 186 and 198.

ANNIE PEREDA
www.fabricademalvaviscos.com
P 56.

AMANDA ALESSI
www.amandaalessi.com
P 199.

ARE WE DESIGNER
www.arewedesigner.com
P 104, 150 and 222.

BILDI GRAFIKS
www.bildi.net
P 62.

BINOCULAR STUDIO
www.binocularstudio.es
P 32 and 230.

BLACK SQUID DESIGN
www.blacksquid.com.au
P 91.

BRAVO COMPANY
www.bravo-company.info
P 208 and 216

BUNCH DESIGN
www.bunchdesign.com
P 102 and 103.

BUREAU RABENSTEINER
www.bureaurabensteiner.at
P 211.

CEES
www.cmontwerp.nl
P 248.

CHRISTINE WISNIESKI
www.christinewisnieski.com
P 6.

D-STUDIO
www.d-studio.co.uk
P 36 and 246.

DEREK BROAD
www.derekbroad.com
P 154.

DESPINA AERAKI
www.aeraki.gr
P 90, 180, 190 and 218.

DONICA IDA
www.donicaida.com
P 14 and 182.

DORIAN
www.estudiodorian.com
P 52.

EL CALOTIPO
www.elcalotipo.com
P 142 and 206.

FERNANDA PORTO
www.thecreativemethod.com
P 242

FRANCESCA PERANI
www.francescaperani.com
P 148, 194 and 240.

GHOST
www.ghostokc.com
P 25 and 72.

GUMMY INDUSTRIES
www.gummyindustries.com
P 34.

HAPPY CENTRO
www.happycentro.it
P 24.

IS CREATIVE STUDIO
www.iscreativestudio.com
P 54, 166, 192 and 200.

JOHN SHEPHERD
www.unsworthshepherd.com
P 92, 94 and 252.

K D DIXON
www.fromkeetra.com
P 60.

KANELLA
www.kanella.com
P 144 and 146.

LA CAJA DE TIPOS
www.lacajadetipos.com
P 137, 138 and 220.

U R INVITED
© 2014 Basheer Graphic Books
© 2014 Mista Studio by Louis Bou

xxxxxxxxxxx

First published in 2014 by:
Basheer Graphic Books,
Blk 13, Toa Payoh, Lorong 8,
#06-08, Braddell Tech
Singapore 319261
t: (65) 6336 0810 f: (65) 6259 1608


Author: Louis Bou
Original idea: Basheer Graphic Books
Design and layout: Àngel Coll
Editor and projects selection: Àngel Coll
Text and art direction: Louis Bou

ISBN: 978-981-07-8865-0

Printed in China, 2014

All images are courtesy of the contributors